SALT & PEPPER SHAKERS II
Identification and Values

Helene Guarnaccia

**Photographs by Michael La Chioma
Proprietor: Hot Shots, Stratford, CT**

COLLECTOR BOOKS
A Division of Schroeder Publishing Co., Inc.

Dedication

This book is dedicated to you, the readers, without whom there would be no reason for this second book. To salt and pepper shaker collectors everywhere—to the never-ending search, the excitement of that wonderful find, and to the absolute joy and fun of discovery. For this is truly a fun hobby—or perhaps a contagious disease!

Please keep writing; your letters have been appreciated more than I can say. I love hearing about your collections, your enthusiasm, and your good wishes. Please write with corrections; there is so much to learn about our mutual interest—and so few places for information. You are my best and greatest resource. Thank you.

Additional copies of this book may be ordered from:

Collector Books
P.O. Box 3009
Paducah, KY 42001

@$14.95. Add $2.00 for postage and handling.

Copright: Helen Guarnaccia, 1989

This book or any part thereof may not be reproduced
without the written consent of the Author and Publisher.

Printed and bound in Singapore by Singapore National Printers Ltd. through Four Colour Imports, Ltd., Louisville, Kentucky.

Table of Contents

Photograph by Ron Lindholm, New York City.

Introduction

Common salt has had tremendous importance throughout history. The Bible says "Ye are the salt of the earth." Slavic people traditionally gave bread and salt as gifts to a bride and groom. Jews exchanged salt to seal a pact; the Greeks and Romans salted sacrifices. Even today in the Roman Catholic Church, salt is the symbol of purity and is placed in the mouth at baptism.

Roman soldiers "worth their salt" were paid a *salary*. The word comes from "salarium," the money paid to soldiers to buy salt. The French Revolution was started, in part, because of the hated salt tax. Spilling salt was considered unlucky by the Romans, and is still so considered today.[1] Evil can be warded off, according to superstition, by throwing a pinch of the spilled salt over the left shoulder with the right hand. In his painting, "The Last Supper," Leonardo da Vinci put an overturned salt cellar in front of Judas to identify him. To be "beneath the salt" at a medieval banquet was indicative of one's low position in society. Those higher up on the social scale sat at the table above the salt cellar. It is still not uncommon to put salt in a coffin; Satan hates salt for it is the symbol of immortality and incorruption. In Scotland, it was customary to throw a handful of salt on the mash when brewing to keep the witches from it.[2]

The earliest containers made to hold salt were used to show off the owner's wealth. They were made of silver and gold. As early as the 16th century, Benvenuto Cellini designed an opulent salt boat of gold, enamel, and ebony. The elaborate container attests to the high value placed on salt. In poor homes salt was stored in wooden troughs called trenchers.

In the early 18th century, pedestal salt dishes were first used. Pepper was one of the spices introduced from the East in the 17th century. Since pepper was used along with many other spices, the casters in which it was kept were called "kitchen peppers." These had a pierced top and were shaped like tankards. It wasn't until early in the 19th century that matched sets of salts and peppers first began to appear.[3] Salt containers were open dishes since the salt absorbed too much moisture to flow freely through a shaker top. The first U.S. patent for a mechanism in a bottle for breaking up and pulverizing salt was issued in 1863, and in 1901 a patent was issued to an Englishman to render common table salt less liable to absorb moisture from the atmosphere.[4]

The salt and pepper shakers pictured in this book were made in the 20th century. There are literally thousands of shakers available; the materials used are myriad; plastic, bakelite, china, pottery, wood, glass, silver, brass, cast iron, and pot metal.

In the 1940's and 1950's, Salt and Pepper Clubs proliferated. One of these was the National Salt and Pepper Club. The club was based in Denver, Colorado and membership cost $1.00. The membership included a subscription to the Club bulletin; their salt and pepper shakers cost $1.00 per pair, or 6 pairs for $5.00! There were also many gift catalogs offering salt and pepper shakers in novelty forms. Many of these were made in the United States, and some were hand painted. Many, of course, were made in Japan, and a very special group stamped "Occupied Japan" was made during the United States Occupation of Japan from the end of World War II until April 28, 1952 when the occupation ended.[5]

Collecting salt and pepper shakers is a bit like eating peanuts (salted, of course). WARNING: Collecting may be habit-forming . . . Have fun!

[1] Gordon Young, "The Essence of Life—Salt" *National Geographic,* Vol. 152. #3, (Sept. 1977), pp. 381-401.

[2] E. Cobham Brewer, *Brewer's Dictionary of Phrase and Fable,* P. 794.

[3] Roger Ashford, "English Silver Salts and Peppers," *The Antiques Journal,* (April 1980), pp. 21-23.

[4] Arthur G. Peterson, *Salt and Salt Shakers,* pp. 7-12.

[5] Gene Florence, *The Collector's Encyclopedia of Occupied Japan Collectibles,* Forward, and p. 50.

Advertising & Promotion

TOP: Elmer and Elsie. Borden Company, 1940's. These have become extremely scarce, and consequently have gone up in price, $25.00-35.00.

CENTER: New York State Thruway. Metal stand trimmed with golf clubs and painted pale green. The golf balls are also metal, $20.00-25.00. New York World's Fair, 1964. These are much less common than the blue and white globes, $20.00-25.00.

BOTTOM: Ceramic Greyhound Buses, $20.00-25.00. RCA Nipper dogs. These are not as fine as the Lenox china set, $10.00-15.00.

TOP: Metal Greyhound buses. These are different from the set pictured in Melva Davern's book. These seem to be later because they are made in Japan. The salt has corroded the paint on one. They have white tops and have the Greyhound logo in blue. I have seen these at antique shows for as much as $50.00. Depending on the condition, $25.00-35.00. Plastic Nipper and gramaphone. These are from the 50's and are marked on the bottom, RCA trademark, $15.00-20.00.

CENTER: 7-Up bottles. These have metal caps, $8.00-10.00. Kellogg's Rice Krispies. Snap and Pop (no crackle), $20.00-25.00.

BOTTOM: Plastic G.E. refrigerators. The old and the new. These are tan and cream, made for Aluminum Housewares Company. The new set shows the ice maker on the outside of the door. I have only seen these twice, $20.00-25.00. Mixmaster. This is the only one I have ever seen with a clear plastic bowl and silver color base. All the others I've seen have been white with black trim, $15.00.

TOP: This "Flour Fred" set is from England. This set, which advertises flour, consists of salt, pepper, mustard, and a pie bird, $15.00-25.00.

CENTER: Blue Nun wine, $10.00-15.00.

BOTTOM: The tiger may be Tony the Tiger. It is a one piece shaker, $5.00-6.00. These Dutch girls are marked "Dairy Queen, trademark" on the back, $10.00-15.00.

TOP: These are the small size Mr. Peanuts. They come in many colors as well as gold and silver and are very common. There are also larger shakers as well as many other collectibles advertising Planters, $4.00-6.00. Gas pumps were given at service stations and often carry the name of the station giving them away on the back. Esso, Texaco and Mobil are the most common, at least in the East. This pair was in the original box, $10.00-15.00

CENTER: Martinis anyone? Le Jon sweet and dry Vermouth, $5.00-8.00. Regina wine and champagne vinegar, $6.00-8.00.

BOTTOM: Volkswagon bus. I bought this brand new in a gift shop in 1985, but I have never seen it again anywhere. It was $12.00 new. I would now value it at between $18.00-25.00 as it was probably not made again.

TOP: Magic Chef plastic chefs, $8.00-10.00. Waring Blenders. Very realistic. I have seen them with yellow, red and black tops, $10.00-15.00.

CENTER: Coke cans, metal. Relatively new, $5.00-7.00. Hershey's Milk Chocolate "mugs", $10.00-12.00.

BOTTOM: Hershey Kisses. Look good enough to eat, $8.00-10.00. Hershey's un-sweetened baking chocolate. Very realistic, $10.00-12.00.

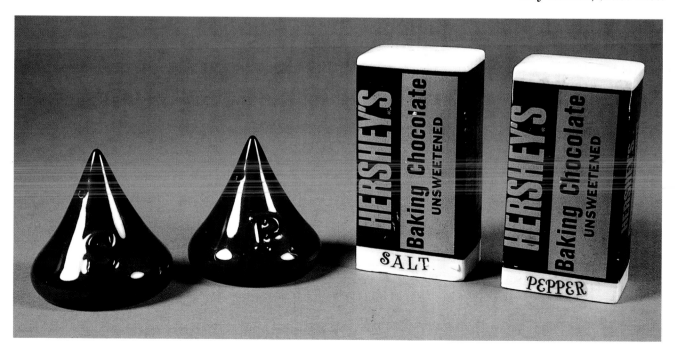

TOP: **Plastic Heinz ketchup bottles, 1970's, $6.00-8.00. Luzianne Mammy. This set is a reproduction. The originals had green skirts. Even these, however, have some value, $10.00-12.00.**

BOTTOM: **Campbell Kids. These are plastic, from the 1950's, and very desirable, $22.00-28.00. Snow shaker. The salt and pepper are on the sides, and the top slides over to reveal the shaker holes. This set is advertising a Sears Kenmore Washer and Dryer—so of course when shaken, it is not snow, but soap suds in the water! This was given away advertising America's largest selling washer and dryer; it was made by the Cooks Corporation in Hong Kong. It has appeal to advertising collectors, salt and pepper shaker collectors and to snow shaker collectors, $15.00-25.00.**

TOP: Bert and Harry Piel, 1970's. Very scarce, $25.00-30.00. Sandeman port wine. These shakers are miniatures of the wine decanter made by Wedgewood for Sandeman, $25.00-30.00.

CENTER: Schlitz beer cans in cardboard holder. Budweiser bottles in box. These have plastic tops and are new, $5.00-7.00.

BOTTOM: Sunshine Bakers. Tiny ceramic shakers with Sunshine incised on hats, $10.00-12.00 Poppin' and Poppie Fresh, the Pillsbury doughboys, plastic, $8.00-10.00.

TOP: Ritz-E sparkling beverages. Bill's Novelty beer and the Mason jars all have metal caps and are older than those with plastic caps. The Bill's set is a souvenir of Milwaukee. The Mobil Oil cans are collected by both salt and pepper shaker collectors and by gasoline and automotive collectors, $8.00-10.00 each pair.

CENTER: These three sets of bottles are old. The first set shows the Statue of Liberty and Rockefeller Center. The second shows a 1940's type bathing beauty on the shore. This one is marked Muth, Buffalo. The third set is 7-Up bottles with metal caps, $8.00-10.00.

BOTTOM: This is an unusual Mr. Peanuts set because it is ceramic, $10.00-12.00. Coppertone Sun Tan Lotion: this is the only set I have seen, $12.00-15.00.

13

Animals

TOP: These two pairs of dressed cats are older than most, probably from the 1940's. Many collectors make a separate collection of animals dressed in human clothes, $10.00-12.00 pr.

CENTER: These cats are also dressed up in pale yellow dresses, $6.00-8.00. Tiny cats in fancy hats, $6.00-8.00. These cats are probably from the 1940's also, $8.00-10.00.

BOTTOM: Kittens on the keys. These will appeal both to cat lovers and to those who collect musical instruments, $6.00-8.00.

15

TOP LEFT: The larger black cats are made by the Shafford Company, $8.00. The smaller set has tails for handles. They are on a red clay base, $5.00.

TOP RIGHT: Tall cartoon cats (8″), $5.00-7.00. White cats designed by Holt-Howard, marked 1958. They also are available as just heads. There are cookie jars, creamers and sugars to match. Shakers, $6.00-8.00.

CENTER: Playful gray cats, $5.00-7.00. These sad looking hound dogs are made in Germany by Goebel, $16.00-18.00.

BOTTOM: Black cat with a ball of yarn, $5.00-7.00. Cats talking on the telephone, $6.00-8.00.

TOP LEFT: More cats! There are several animals like these pale yellow outlined in black, $5.00-7.00. Tall stylized black bisque cats, $6.00-8.00. Calico cat and dog playing, $6.00-8.00.

TOP RIGHT: Three pairs of yellow-orange cats, $5.00-7.00.

CENTER: Cat and pillow are each the shaker, $8.00. Dog on pillow, $8.00.

BOTTOM: These are most unusual, at least I have only seen them once. The heads are a shaker; the body is a shaker. The head fits into the body. The dog and the cat are each a separate pair, $10.00-12.00.

TOP: Long stylized black cats by Dan Brechner and Co., Inc., $10.00-12.00. Bone china grayhounds, very nicely detailed, $10.00-12.00.

CENTER: Dog carrier. Two baskets are the shakers, $6.00-8.00. Cartoon type dogs, $6.00-8.00.

BOTTOM: Heavy, nicely crafted dachshunds, $8.00-10.00. St. Bernards, complete with barrels, $10.00-12.00.

TOP: Three sets of black dogs, center set is bisque, $5.00-7.00.

CENTER: This is one of my favorite dog sets. The mother is the mustard pot; the puppies' heads are the salt and pepper, $15.00-18.00. Mother and baby pig, $6.00-8.00.

BOTTOM: This is a complicated set to use. The two sides of the bucket are the salt and pepper. They are held together by inserting the dog on a wire frame, $8.00-10.00. This one piece shaker is really great! The deco dogs are attached together. One has holes in front and one in back on the head, $8.00-10.00.

TOP: There are many dog and dog house combinations. This is Sad Sack. The dog and the house are each a shaker, $8.00-10.00. This is one of many intricate shaker sets where an animal's foot fits into a hole; this time in a basket, $8.00-10.00.

CENTER LEFT: These orange and yellow dogs have a nice glaze. I think they are from the 1940's. The dogs on the right look mean and a little suspicious of the Spaniels on the left, $6.00-8.00.

CENTER RIGHT: The elongated cow paired with the dachshund is a bit of whimsy, $8.00-10.00. The orange and yellow bunnies are similar to the dogs above, $6.00-7.00.

BOTTOM: Another dachshund and cow combination. Why? $8.00-10.00.

TOP: Stylized dogs. The ones on the right look like butterscotch. $6.00-8.00.

BOTTOM: A dachshund split in half, $8.00-10.00. Deco dog and cat, $8.00-10.00.

TOP: This is another of my all time favorites. The details are wonderful. The set is exquisitely made! Both the father and the baby kangaroo are dressed in top hat and tails—imagine the father carrying the baby, $35.00-45.00. Bone china English bull dogs, $10.00-12.00.

CENTER: Plastic Basset Hounds. They sure look sad, $5.00-6.00.

BOTTOM LEFT: Gingham dog and calico cat, $6.00-8.00. Dressed ducks, $6.00-8.00.

BOTTOM RIGHT: Hugging bunnies, $5.00-7.00. Siamese cats with blue rhinestone eyes, $6.00-8.00.

TOP: Ceramic Art Studio, Madison, Wisconsin. These clearly marked shakers are becoming increasingly collectible and going up in price all the time. Siamese cats, $18.00-20.00. Pigs, $15.00-18.00.

CENTER: Ceramic Art Studio. Hare and tortoise, $15.00-18.00. Ceramic Art Studio. The fox and the goose, $15.00-18.00.

BOTTOM: Stylized horses, $6.00-8.00. Very old donkey (1940's, possibly 1930's) with cart full of chickens, $10.00-15.00

TOP LEFT: **Two horses lying down, $6.00-8.00. Italian type donkey pulling cart, $6.00-8.00.**

TOP RIGHT: **Horse heads and bull dogs; both nicely glazed, $7.00-9.00**

CENTER: **Very nice mother and colt heads, $8.00-10.00. Cow with two milk pails, $6.00-8.00.**

BOTTOM: **Ceramic boots, $6.00-7.00. Horse heads on stand with saddle. Saddle is toothpick holder, $8.00-10.00.**

TOP: Rosemeade horse heads. Dark green. The Rosemeade pottery operated in Wahpeton, North Dakota from 1940 until 1961. These horse heads have the rose sticker, $10.00-15.00. Black and white metal rocking horses, Amish type, $6.00-8.00.

CENTER: The prancing horses are bone china. Very nice detail, $10.00-12.00. Giraffes are favorites of many collectors, $6.00-8.00.

BOTTOM: Circus horses, $6.00-8.00. Horse heads marked Kentucky, $6.00-8.00.

TOP: Circus animals. Pale blue with gold trim. Elephants, $6.00-8.00. Monkeys, $6.00-8.00.

CENTER: Circus animals. Monkey on base, $8.00-10.00. Pig is missing bottom of base which is sugar bowl, $8.00-10.00 (complete).

BOTTOM: Circus Animals. Lion on drum, $10.00-12.00. Elephant on circus ball, $10.00-12.00.

26

TOP: **Black horses trimmed in gold. Saddle bags are shakers, $6.00-8.00.**

CENTER: **Mother and baby seal and black bears, $6.00-8.00.**

BOTTOM: **Black ducks and one piece stylized shaker, $6.00-8.00.**

TOP: I bought these three sets in Italy. They are collectible there too! Dogs and monkeys on motorcycles, $10.00-12.00. Bisque pigs in basket, $8.00-10.00.

CENTER: These two sets of ceramic pigs are all dressed up, $8.00-10.00.

BOTTOM: Shawnee large pigs and Mugsy dogs. Shawnee Pottery operated in Zanesville, Ohio from 1937 until 1961, $18.00-22.00. Small Mugsy dog, $10.00-12.00

28

TOP: Tiny musical pigs, $5.00-7.00. Goat playing violin on a rocking chair; goat is one shaker; rocker is the other. Goats are relatively scarce, $10.00-12.00

CENTER: Large and small pigs, $6.00-8.00.

BOTTOM: Male chauvinist pig (probably from the 1970's), $6.00-8.00. Large pig. Design under glaze unlike American Pottery where it is applied on top of glaze & so often washes off, $8.00-10.00.

29

TOP: Paddington Bear. The loveable English character, $12.00-15.00. A wonderful monkey couple. All dressed up, $10.00-12.00.

CENTER: Two Mother and child sets. There were many of these made. Mouse and baby, $8.00-10.00. Monkey and baby, $8.00-10.00.

BOTTOM: Deco Cats. Very stylized, $8.00-10.00. Luster elephants. Also stylized, $8.00-10.00.

TOP: Another stylized elephant set. This one has mustard pot, $15.00-18.00. Two self-satisfied looking pigs, $6.00-8.00.

CENTER: Elephants and pigs decorated with bone china flowers, $6.00-8.00.

BOTTOM: Pigs. Tiny, cartoon type, $5.00-7.00. Large elephants wearing hat and tie, $8.00-10.00.

TOP LEFT: Cartoon type elephants, $6.00-8.00.

CENTER: Three pairs of elephants. One set with trunks down (unusual), $8.00-10.00.

TOP RIGHT: Elephants dressed for the office, $8.00-10.00. Deer, $6.00-8.00.

BOTTOM: Elephant pulling a cart, $8.00-10.00. These giraffes with the twisted necks are wonderful, and it is a miracle that any have survived, $10.00-12.00.

TOP: Very nicely made chick in egg and mother hen, bisque, $10.00-12.00. The upright pig will rest on the other, $5.00-7.00.

CENTER: Cartoon type pigs and cows, $6.00-8.00.

BOTTOM LEFT: Cows with bone china flowers, gold halos, and rhinestones (anyone's guess), $6.00-8.00.

BOTTOM RIGHT: Teddy bear in car. The bear is one shaker. The car the other, $10.00-12.00. Cartoon cows with bells. These are rather charming, $8.00-10.00.

33

TOP: Two birds on swing. These are swingers, $8.00-10.00. Bear and dog. Their arms rest on post and they rock (and roll?), $10.00-12.00.

BOTTOM: Love Bugs by Bendel, designed by Ruth van Tellingen Bendel, $18.00-22.00.

TOP: Cartoon cows, $6.00-8.00. Bisque Brahmin bulls, $8.00-10.00.

CENTER: There are several variations of the rabbit in the top hat. It is , in fact, being reproduced by Vandor, a California Company, $10.00-12.00. The hare and the tortoise. This also has many variations, $8.00-10.00.

BOTTOM: This bunny has more distinct features than the preceding one, $10.00-12.00. These teddy bears come in many different color combinations, $6.00-8.00.

35

TOP: The beetles are anthropomorphic. These are musicians. One holding the music, the other playing the violin, $8.00-10.00. These frogs play leap frog, $6.00-8.00

CENTER LEFT: Large frog and toadstool, $5.00-7.00. Small penguins in top hats, $5.00-7.00.

CENTER RIGHT: Cartoon type frogs in metal tray with umbrellas, $8.00-10.00.

BOTTOM: Musical frogs, and a frog on a lily (?) pad, each pair, $6.00-8.00.

TOP: Gray mice on bread. Colorful mouse on Swiss cheese, $6.00-8.00.

CENTER: Christmas mouse on Swiss cheese, $6.00-7.00. Mouse with foot through hole, intricate, $8.00-10.00. Mouse sitting in bread, $8.00-10.00. Mouse sitting in cheese, $8.00-10.00.

BOTTOM: Mouse with two cheese shakers, $7.00-9.00. Dog is holding two baskets which are the shakers. His head comes off and reveals a mustard pot, $8.00-10.00.

TOP: **Dressed up rabbits. These look like Beatrix Potter characters, $8.00-10.00. Dressed bears are made in Germany, $8.00-12.00.**

CENTER: **Dressed pigs, $6.00-8.00. Two bears on a bicycle built for two, $10.00-12.00.**

BOTTOM: **Zebras and snakes. The odd couple, $8.00-10.00.**

TOP: Kliban's Cat and a pair of well dressed mice (1960's), $8.00-10.00.

CENTER TOP: Both of these pairs of lions are wonderful. The bone china set is realistic, and the other set is comic, $10.00 pr.

CENTER BOTTOM: Nicely detailed hippo and steer-bone china, $8.00-10.00.

BOTTOM: Bear holding two fish which are the salt and pepper, $6.00-8.00. Hippos, $6.00-8.00.

39

TOP: These four pairs of shakers are Luster, an iridescent glaze. Blue rabbits, $6.00-8.00. Camel. The saddle bags are the shakers, $10.00-12.00. Frogs, $6.00-8.00. Toucans, $8.00-10.00.

CENTER: Panda and tree trunk, $6.00-8.00. Rabbits with pocket book and umbrella, $6.00-8.00.

BOTTOM: Black bears. Red clay base, shiny black glaze, $5.00-7.00. Nice penguins, but it looks like someone forgot to paint the feet on one of them, $6.00-8.00.

40

Birds & Fowl

TOP: With the popularity of the "Country" look, chickens and ducks have become very collectible. These three pairs show just some of the tremendous variety. The black and white speckled ones are especially nice, $6.00-8.00 pr.

CENTER: The taller chickens on the right are also egg cups, $7.00-9.00.

BOTTOM: The tiny white chickens in the red metal basket are from Italy. The white and red are most traditional, $6.00-8.00.

TOP: **Turkeys are fun on the table for Thanksgiving. One collector I know collects only those shakers with a holiday theme, and uses them at the appropriate times, $6.00-8.00.**

CENTER: **Chicks in a basket, $6.00-8.00. Stylized chicks with painted flower decoration, $5.00-7.00.**

BOTTOM: **Black chickens (On a red clay base), $4.00-6.00. Egg heads, the graduate and friend, $6.00-8.00.**

TOP LEFT: Tall black and red chickens, $5.00-7.00. Chicken holding two eggs. The eggs are the shakers, $6.00-8.00.

TOP RIGHT: A pair of feisty looking fowl, $6.00-8.00. Small yellow penguins. These also come in pink and blue, $5.00-7.00.

CENTER: These hugging ducks are not old, but nice, $10.00-12.00. Penguins are also very collectible, $8.00-10.00.

BOTTOM LEFT: I could use the help of an ornithologist with these. The pair on the right might be a wood duck, but after searching through three bird books I'm still not sure. They're bisque and nicely colored, $8.00-10.00.

BOTTOM RIGHT: More ducks. The pair on the right are mallard, $6.00-8.00.

TOP: Cartoon ducks, $6.00-8.00.

CENTER: Cartoon ducks shouting at a pair of ostriches. The latter are unusual. Ducks, $6.00-8.00. Ostriches, $10.00-12.00.

BOTTOM: Dressed up ducks on tray, $6.00-8.00. Very ornate basket with two chicks, old and lovely, $10.00-12.00.

TOP: Realistic bisque birds. Baltimore Orioles, $8.00-10.00. Blue Jays, $8.00-10.00.

CENTER: These clay ducks are from Mexico. They are rather crudely made, but charming. The pair on the right are a form of toucans, $5.00-7.00.

BOTTOM: Ducks in different positions, $6.00-8.00.

TOP LEFT: The penguins on the left are a combination of white swirled glass and black plastic. In original box, $10.00-12.00. The penguins on the right are quite tall and made of plastic, $6.00-8.00.

TOP RIGHT: Tiny penguins in hats and bow ties, $6.00-8.00. Penguins in chef hats, $8.00-10.00.

CENTER: These are both nice ceramic penguins, $8.00-10.00.

BOTTOM: Red-head or canvas back ducks, $8.00-10.00. Penguin dressed in his formal, $8.00-10.00.

TOP: **Two pairs of flamingos and a pair of pelicans. Flamingos have become extremely collectible and are being widely reproduced. They recall the era of Art Deco which is so popular today, $10.00-15.00.**

CENTER: **These flamingos are extremely graceful and delicate, $12.00-15.00.**

BOTTOM: **A pair of flamingos is often depicted with one head up and one down, $12.00-15.00. Fish with the same vivid pink coloration, $6.00-8.00.**

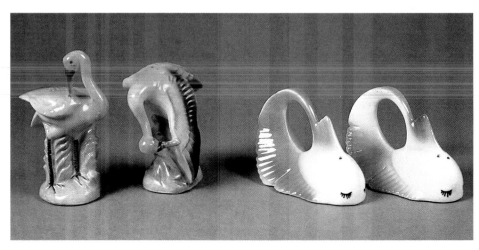

TOP: **Flamingos, $10.00-12.00. Birds hanging by their tails from a branch, $7.00-9.00.**

BOTTOM: **Flamingo with palm tree, $15.00-18.00. Cormorants (?), $6.00-8.00.**

49

TOP: Owls have long been collectible, and there are several owl collectors' clubs. Tiny pair on tree trunk, $6.00-8.00. Cartoon type owls, $5.00-7.00. Owls, $5.00-7.00.

CENTER: Luster owls, $6.00-8.00; Luster birds, $6.00-8.00.

BOTTOM: Two more pairs of cartoon type owls, $5.00-7.00.

50

TOP LEFT: The birds on the left are made in Germany, $8.00-10.00. Small birds, $5.00-7.00.

TOP RIGHT: Large luster birds with gold trim, $6.00-8.00. Sleek red birds. These are heavy and modern looking, $7.00-9.00.

CENTER: Both these pairs of birds are nice quality bisque. Green parrots, $8.00-10.00. Red Cardinals, $8.00-10.00.

BOTTOM LEFT: Swans, $6.00-8.00. Road runners, $6.00-8.00.

BOTTOM RIGHT: Colorful birds, $5.00-7.00. Bone china birds fit into branch, $6.00-8.00.

TOP: These elegant blue and white birds are stamped U.S.S.R. and are the only shakers I've had from Russia, $15.00-18.00. Brown bird, $5.00-7.00.

CENTER: Ring-necked Pheasants. These are very common, $5.00-7.00.

BOTTOM: Toucans. There are many variations of these. I just love them; partly because they are comical, but mostly because they are so brightly colored, $6.00-10.00. Collection of Barbara Young, Fairfield, CT.

Black Americana

Salt and pepper shakers depicting black people have not been made since the Civil Rights Movement. Since they have been somewhat scarce, they have increased in value. Recently, however, some black people salt and pepper shakers have been reproduced. They are quite obviously new; generally the newer ceramics are lighter in weight, the colors are brighter and they have a different "feel." Of course, they too will become collectible in time, but their intial price should be considerably lower.

TOP: There are many stereotypical sets of blacks with watermelons. These are two separate pairs. In each set, the watermelon is one shaker, and the boy the other. The larger set is about 5½″ tall, $25.00-35.00.

BOTTOM: There are two pairs of boys with watermelons like the preceding set, but these are smaller, $22.00-28.00. The small chubby boy is eating one piece of watermelon, and the other, larger piece is the other shaker, $25.00-30.00. The girl in the green plaid dress is a single, has anyone seen her mate? $10.00-15.00.

TOP: Another variation of the boy with watermelon, $28.00-32.00. The colors in this set are wonderful. The man's hat and the watermelon are a vivid red-orange, $25.00-35.00.

CENTER: The black boy riding the camel is not an American Black, but probably Indian, $25.00-35.00. The chef carrying two slices of watermelons on trays is unusual, $25.00-35.00.

BOTTOM: There are many salt and pepper shakers depicting black children riding various vegetables. These two are eggplants and carrots, $22.00-28.00.

TOP: These children are on a pair of pea pods, $22.00-28.00. This black boy is riding on a whale. There is a knob on the whale's back and an indentation in the boy, so that he sits securely without fear of falling, $25.00-39.00.

CENTER: This set is one of the Van Tellingen "Huggers." This is a black boy hugging a puppy. There is also a white boy hugging the same puppy, $28.00-32.00. Another vegetable set. This one is heads of lettuce, $22.00-28.00.

BOTTOM: There are many chef and mammy sets. In both of these, they are holding cooking utensils, $16.00-22.00.

TOP: The blue and red set comes in many sizes. There is also a matching vinegar and oil cruet set shown in my last book, $16.00-22.00. The short fat mammy and chef are fun and funny.There are many variations on these, $18.00-22.00.

BOTTOM: This is the Pearl China mammy and chef. These are the large ones, $35.00-45.00. There is also a matching cookie jar. These small heads with chef hats are made from nuts and cork, $8.00-10.00.

TOP: This is a cruet set. The larger pair are for vinegar and oil. The heads are attached to cork stoppers. The smaller set is the salt and pepper. 4 pieces, $45.00-55.00.

CENTER: Two boys shooting dice. The dice are attached to the tray, $30.00-35.00. Small boys with round mouths and bright orange hats, $25.00-30.00.

BOTTOM: Wooden porter. The two suitcases are the shakers, $22.00-25.00. Boy on toilet. Each is a shaker, $25.00-28.00

TOP: African chieftan heads with fancy headdresses, $18.00-20.00. Boy and girl heads with chef hat and bow, $20.00-24.00.

CENTER: Ceramic Art Studio. Ethiopian Guards, $28.00-32.00.

BOTTOM: Both of these sets are Eastern since they are wearing turbans, $12.00-15.00.

59

TOP: **This is an extraordinary set I bought in England. It represents the beloved English character of storybook and doll fame known as the Golliwog. The character is currently the logo for Robertson's jam and marmalade. This set was commissioned by them in the 1970's. In addition to the salt, pepper, toothpick holder and toast rack shown, there was a sugar bowl in the shape of a piano and a tea pot and creamer. Salt and pepper set, $22.00-25.00.**

CENTER: **Native women with baskets of fruit. Probably Carribean, $22.00-28.00.**

BOTTOM: **African tribal couple complete with shields, $22.00-28.00. American black chef and cook, $25.00-30.00. Native children, $22.00-25.00.**

TOP: Wooden chef with salt and pepper pots, $18.00-22.00.

BOTTOM: The position of this boy's legs looks like he's about to take off and do a dance! I have seen this set in several variations; usually with a German looking beer-meister. This set is rare, $45.00-55.00.

Ceramic Novelty

LEFT: This old car with salt dish, pepper shaker and mustard pot has a postcard type scene of Brighton Beach on its side. It is a souvenir set and made of lusterware, $25.00-30.00.

LEFT CENTER: San Francisco cable cars. These also come in green and in a copper colored metal, $6.00-8.00. Racing cars, $6.00-8.00.

RIGHT CENTER: This light blue train is a four piece set. Complete, $18.00-24.00.

BOTTOM: This two piece trailer truck says S & P Co. on the side, $8.00-12.00. These 1918 Fords are metal and made like toy cars, $15.00-18.00.

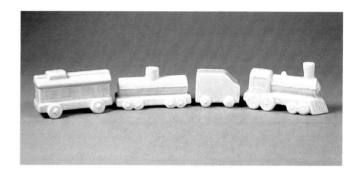

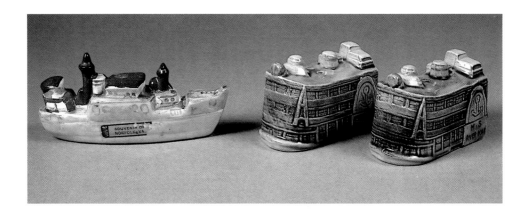

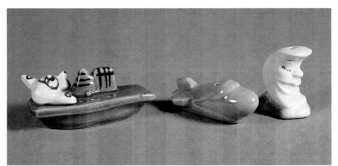

TOP: **The boat on left has removable smoke stacks, $6.00-8.00. The Sidewinder riverboats have a paddle wheel, $6.00-8.00.**

CENTER: **The penguin pulling a trailer is driving a pretty sporty car, and his lady friend is watching out the window, $12.00-15.00. Two piece telephone. The receiver is one shaker, the base the other, $12.00-15.00.**

UPPER BOTTOM: **Aircraft carrier and plane, $10.00-15.00. Rocket and moon, $10.00-15.00.**

LOWER BOTTOM: **Sailboat and light house on tray, $8.00-10.00. Bright colored smiling tugs, $8.00-10.00.**

64

TOP LEFT: Another sailboat and light house on tray, $8.00-10.00. Airplanes, $8.00-12.00.

TOP RIGHT: Metal car with two ceramic figures which are the salt and pepper, $10.00-12.00. Three sail boats. One is the handle attached to the tray, $8.00-10.00.

UPPER CENTER: The man is holding on to the toilet chain. Around the bowl it says "Goodbye cruel world", $18.00-25.00. These same racing cars with moveable metal wheels have many different names on the labels. Connaught, Mercedes, Benz, etc., $12.00-15.00.

LOWER CENTER: Bus and fire engine with people faces, $10.00-12.00. This car is quite amazing. It all comes apart. The front is the pepper, the back the salt, and the man (with spoon attached), is the top to the mustard pot, $15.00-18.00.

BOTTOM: A "Streetcar Named Desire" marked New Orleans, $6.00-8.00. Stanley Steamer and Ford T 1908, $10.00-12.00.

Houses - I put these around a table-top Christmas tree and had Santa Claus salt and peppers all around. It made a charming Christmas village.

TOP: A beehive house, English cottages, and a cylinder shape, $6.00-8.00.

CENTER: Log cabins, $6.00-8.00. The roofs of these say "God Bless Our Mortgaged Home," $8.00-10.00. These orange roofed houses are quite charming, $6.00-8.00.

BOTTOM: This set is absolutely gorgeous. It was made by Noritake and is extremely fine, $20.00-30.00.

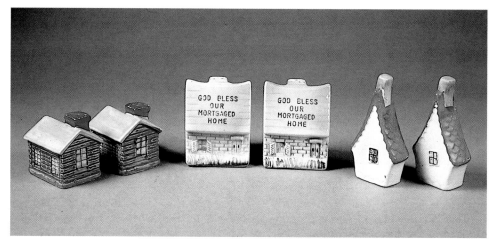

TOP: Two pairs of English type houses and a windmill, $6.00-8.00.

CENTER: These are Delft windmills. The blades move and are metal, $8.00-10.00.

BOTTOM: Tiny luster houses on tray, light house, and lady and open salt, $8.00-10.00.

TOP LEFT: **Footballs, very realistic looking. $6.00-8.00. Tennis racket and ball, $6.00-8.00.**

TOP RIGHT: **Golf club and ball, $8.00-10.00. Golf ball and bag, $8.00-10.00.**

UPPER CENTER: **Boxing gloves, $6.00-8.00. Pool balls, $8.00-10.00.**

LOWER CENTER: **These sport sets in metal frames are marked Shafford, Japan with a paper sticker. There is no mark on the shaker. They are very well made. Basketball and soccer, $12.00-15.00**

BOTTOM: **Baseball, football and golf, $12.00-15.00.**

Go-Withs - these were described to me as a pair consisting of two unlike pieces that go together as bacon "goes with" eggs.

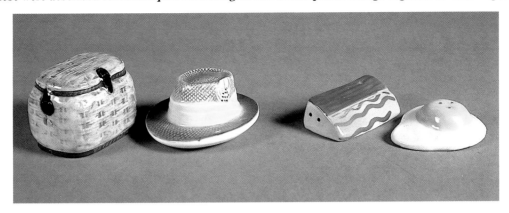

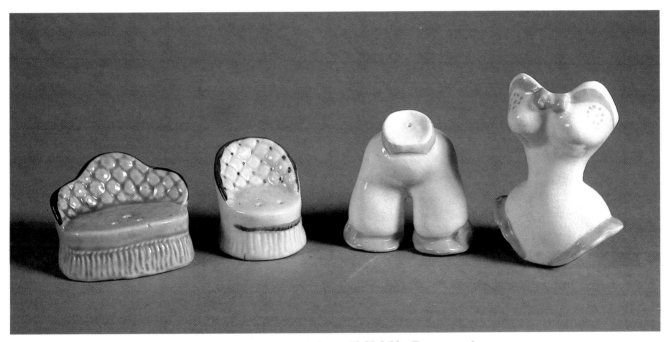

TOP: Fishing creel and hat, $6.00-8.00. Bacon and eggs, $8.00-10.00.

CENTER: Chair and sofa, $8.00-10.00. Bodice and pantaloons, $8.00-10.00.

BOTTOM: Telephone and directory (this also comes in black and tan), $8.00-10.00. Lipstick and perfume bottle, $8.00-10.00.

69

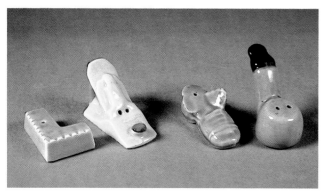

TOP: **Tire and Nail, $8.00-10.00. Hitchhiker and bag, $8.00-10.00.**
CENTER LEFT: **Plane and square, $8.00-10.00. Pipe and slipper, $8.00-10.00.**
CENTER RIGHT: **Hammer and bruised thumb, $8.00-10.00. Lock and key, $8.00-10.00.**
BOTTOM: **Typewriter and Ink, $8.00-10.00. Typewriter "People," $10.00-12.00.**

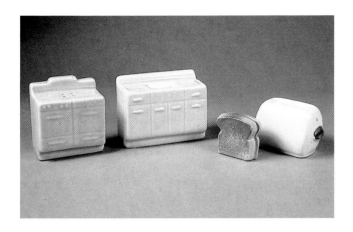

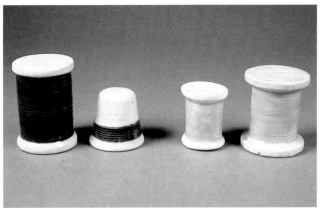

Household - I have heard from several collectors who furnish doll houses with salt and pepper shaker furniture and accessories.

TOP LEFT: **Kitchen sink and stove,** $8.00-10.00. **Toaster and toast,** $6.00-8.00.

TOP RIGHT: **Thimble and thread,** $6.00-8.00. **Large and small thread,** $6.00-8.00.

CENTER: **Sewing machine on base,** $10.00-12.00. **Two-piece camera,** $10.00-12.00.

BOTTOM: **Refrigerator. This is a single. It may go with a chef,** $5.00. **Coffee grinders,** $5.00-7.00.

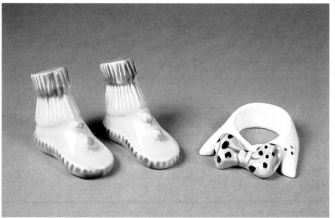

TOP LEFT: Water faucets, $8.00-10.00. Binoculars, $8.00-10.00.

TOP RIGHT: Slipper socks, $8.00-10.00. Collar and bow tie, $8.00-10.00.

CENTER: Spoons and forks. These "people things" also come in dishes, pots, pans and clocks, $8.00-10.00.

BOTTOM LEFT: Pot bellied stove, $6.00-8.00. Irons, $6.00-8.00.

BOTTOM RIGHT: Piano and bench, $6.00-8.00. Guitar and mandolin, $8.00-10.00.

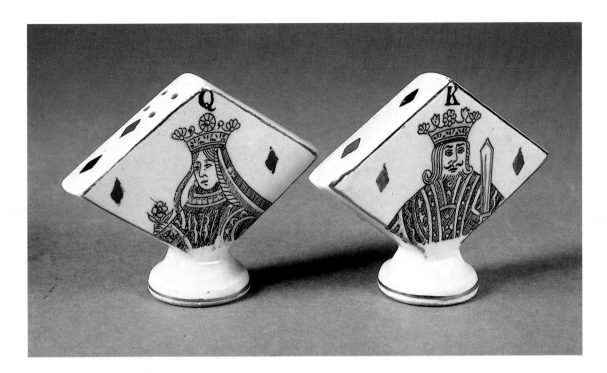

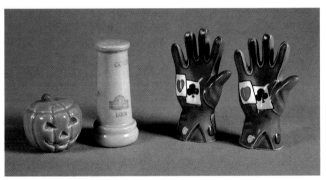 

TOP: For card lovers: A king and queen of diamonds, $6.00-8.00.
CENTER LEFT: Pumpkin and cylinder saying: "October-Libra, Parkcraft, $12.00-15.00—one of a series of 12 months, each cylinder has a corresponding symbol. A pair of gloves decorated with club and heart, $8.00-10.00.
CENTER RIGHT: These are very unusual. Two sets makes faces. The middle set is just an abstract puzzle, $12.00-15.00.
BOTTOM: Pick and shovel. Road signs. Cautions against using too much salt and pepper, $8.00-10.00.

TOP: Hats. The man with the bib, fork and spoon has taken his hat off to salt his food. His head is the other shaker, $10.00-12.00. The brightly colored men's hats are Occupied Japan, $15.00-18.00.

CENTER: Civil war hats, $8.00-10.00. Pilgrim hats, $7.00-9.00.

BOTTOM: Shriner hats, marked Temple Treasures, F.N. Kistner, Chicago, 441307, $10.00-12.00.

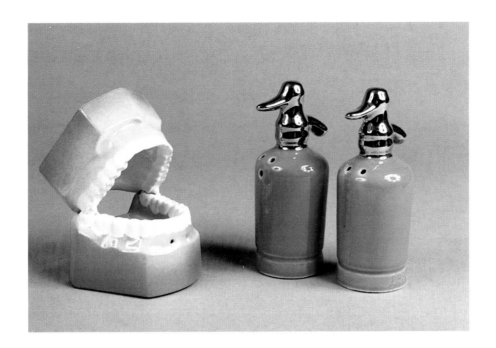

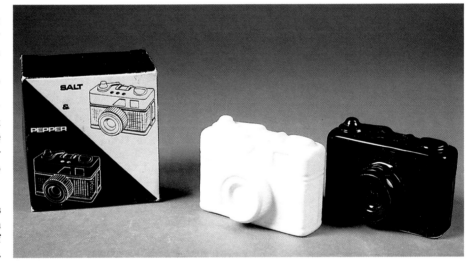

TOP: False teeth (a perfect gift for your dentist), $10.00-12.00. Seltzer bottles, $8.00-10.00.

CENTER: Black and white cameras, a striking pair, $8.00-10.00.

BOTTOM: Pipes and feet, both souvenirs of Maine, $6.00-8.00.

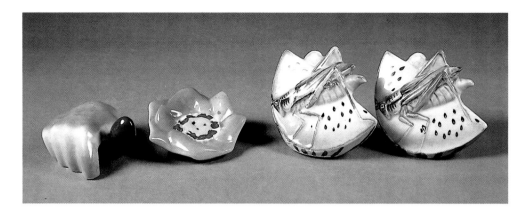

TOP: Green thumb and flower, $6.00-8.00. Grasshoppers on watermelon slices, $6.00-8.00.

CENTER: A scholarly cat with "Salt and Pepper, Vol. VIII," $6.00-8.00. In case the pun wasn't clear, these books are marked "book worm," $6.00-8.00.

BOTTOM: These three "range" sets are handsome, and to think they came with the stove in the good old days, $10.00-12.00.

76

TOP LEFT: **Dice trimmed with gold**, $6.00-8.00. These binoculars are luster-ware, elegant, $8.00-10.00.

TOP RIGHT: **Plastic nuns**, $3.00-5.00. **Bible and organ**, $6.00-8.00.

UPPER CENTER: **Grand Ole Opry souvenir set**, $6.00-8.00. **Violin and case**, $8.00-10.00.

LOWER CENTER: **Boots and hat**, $6.00-8.00. **Two halves of a mailbox**, $6.00-8.00.

BOTTOM: **Old fashioned telephone, two types**, $6.00-8.00. **Boxing gloves and bag**, $6.00-8.00.

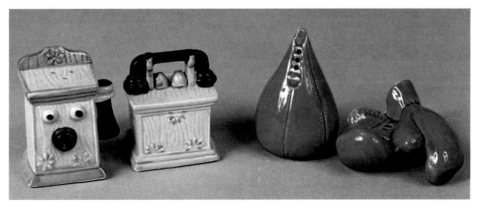

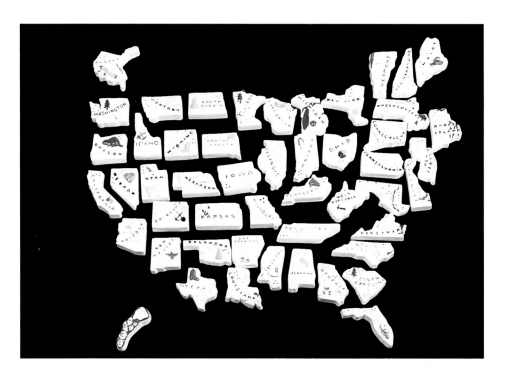

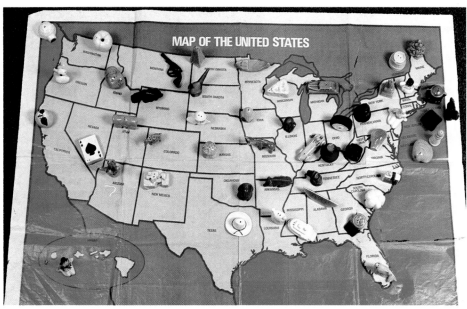

TOP: The 50 states of the United States. These are the states made by Parkcraft. The states are not in proportion. Note the relative size of Texas and Connecticut. The products or symbols of each state are in the next picture. Price is per pair, i.e., state and symbol, $10.00-15.00.

CENTER: The state symbols are placed on their respective state locations. Note Hawaii and Alaska. Priced as pair with state. There are two different sets, one with several of the symbols repeated. Several states have a cotton ball, sheaf of wheat, etc. This set is from the 1940's. In the 1950's and 1960's, Parkcraft made the set as shown here with each symbol different. This complete list is given in my last book on page 169.

BOTTOM: These states are not Parkcraft. They are a matched pair of two identical states. Nebraska, $6.00-8.00. Rhode Island, $3.00-5.00.

Many salt and pepper sets include a tray and/or a mustard pot. These sets generally command a higher price. In England they are called condiment sets, *not* salt & peppers.

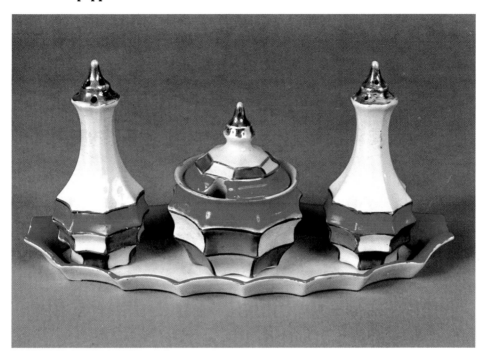

TOP: **This attractive set is very colorful, $18.00-25.00.**

BOTTOM: **The elephants, turtles and eggs I bought in Italy. Note the shape of the tray repeating the animal shape. Elephants and turtles on tray, $15.00-20.00. Pink and blue egg, $6.00-8.00.**

TOP: The luster fish and tomato set is marvelous. It is definitely pre-war; possibly from the 1930's. The boar (?) is another souvenir set with a postcard type view reproduced on the china. These are very collectible, $25.00-30.00.

CENTER: A luster tray and mustard set. Each side represents a swan, $20.00. There are many pretty Japanese salt and pepper shakers that are gold trimmed or glazed in a luster finish. These are pretty rather than novel, and thus not really the subject of this book, $8.00-10.00.

BOTTOM: Two flowers in a luster tray, $8.00-10.00. Two crowns on a tray, $6.00-8.00.

Christmas

TOP: Christmas mice atop wedges of Swiss cheese. These squeak when turned over, $8.00-10.00. Santa and his reindeer are taking a nap. Good thing they didn't all try to get into that bed, $10.00-12.00.

CENTER: This little Santa and tree look very old and charming, $10.00-12.00. Two cartoon type reindeer, not so old, $6.00-8.00.

BOTTOM: These stylized Snowmen on the Christmas tree-shaped tray were bought at the same time and place as the turtles and elephants on trays, $15.00-20.00.

82

TOP: Two jolly pairs of Santas. The ones with the "gingerbread" trim are older. They have bright blue eyes, $10.00-12.00. Imagine using shakers over your food that have real whiskers. Surely these were made just for show, $10.00-12.00.

CENTER: Mr. and Mrs. Santa in their rocking chairs, $10.00-12.00. This next pair is not a pair. I think the Santa goes with the reindeer in the next photo (note dark green holly leaves). Mrs. Santa might go with the Santa in the light green chair. There are so many Christmas sets. The older ones should be $10.00-12.00 per pair.

BOTTOM: These snowmen have a flat bisque type finish, $8.00-10.00. The two Santas in the middle of this photo are very old, $12.00-15.00. Two gaily gift wrapped packages, $6.00-8.00.

TOP: A cheerful looking pair. Mr. and Mrs. Snowman bearing gifts, $8.00-10.00. A shiny pair of black boots for Christmas, $5.00-7.00.

BOTTOM: These four sets are brand new (1986) but probably will not be made again. The ducks with Christmas ribbons reflect the country look in decorating so popular this year. The kissing and hugging Santas are sweet, and the trees are just the right size for a doll house, $8.00-12.00.

Fantasy, Fables & Fairy Tales

TOP: **Mary and her lamb,
$12.00-15.00. Mother Goose,
who started the whole thing,
with her house and her very
own goose, $15.00-18.00.**

CENTER: **Little Boy Blue and
his haystack, $12.00-15.00. The
old woman who lived in the
shoe, $10.00-12.00.**

BOTTOM: **Little Miss Muffet
(Relco pottery), $18.00-20.00.
The cat and the Fiddle,
$10.00-12.00.**

86

TOP: These three sets are all part of the same series. They all have the name written on the bottom of their skirt and were made by Relco. Red Riding Hood, Mary Had a Little Lamb, and the Queen of Hearts, $18.00-20.00.
CENTER: The central figure here is the mouse who ran up the clock, $10.00-12.00. The others are all story book characters, $8.00-10.00.
BOTTOM: There are probably more examples of Humpty Dumpty than any other character in children's fiction. Most are sitting on a wall. These are just some of the many examples, $8.00-10.00.

TOP: These almost look like the vegetable and fruit people, $6.00-8.00.

CENTER: The pair on the extreme right look hand painted and may have been made from a mold in a ceramics class, $6.00-8.00.

BOTTOM: The background pair are 8½″ tall. One has on pants, one a skirt. The first time I've heard of a male and female Humpty (1952), $6.00-10.00.

88

TOP: Mickey Mouse and Minnie. This set is quite rare and is from the 1950's. There may be many of them in the hands of collectors, but they certainly are not out in the marketplace, $25.00-35.00.

CENTER: A pair of bells from Disneyland, obviously much newer than Mickey and Minnie, $6.00-8.00. Here Mickey and Minnie are seated on a bench marked WD52 (the year), $25.00-35.00.

BOTTOM LEFT: The Hull Red Riding Hood. This is the 3½" size. There is also a 5½" size, $18.00-22.00. Mickey Mouse and Minnie dressed as Mr. & Mrs. Claus, $15.00-18.00.

BOTTOM RIGHT: A wonderful Pinocchio, but unfortunately a single, $12.00-15.00. American Pottery Company Dumbo. On the back of these Walt Disney is impressed. There is no color to the print and sometimes you have to hold it up to the light to see it, $12.00-15.00.

89

TOP: **More American Pottery Walt Disney characters, Pluto and Dumbo. This time trimmed in red. These paints are *not* under glaze, so do not scrub! Walt Disney mark is at base, $12.00-15.00.**

CENTER: **American Pottery Mickey and Minnie and Tweetie Bird(?), $12.00-15.00.**

BOTTOM: **A beautiful set of Snow White and one of the Seven Dwarfs. I don't know if any of the others were made in salt and pepper shakers. I have seen the whole set in figurines, $20.00-25.00.**

90

TOP: Great cartoon characters: Yosemite Sam, Tweetie Bird, Sylvester and Bugs and Bunny, $20.00-25.00.

CENTER: Winnie the Pooh and Rabbit, $20.00-25.00. This character is called "Adamson," the best known Swedish comic strip, created in 1920 by Oscar Jacobsson. The stocky little man was bald except for three hairs sticking up on his head, and he constantly smoked a cigar. In 1922, this strip became "Silent Sam," and was the first Scandinavian comic strip published in the United States, $18.00-22.00.

BOTTOM: Maggie and Jiggs, very scarce, $30.00-35.00.

TOP: The middle set is Snoopy from "Charlie Brown" by Charles Schulz, $6.00-8.00. Moon Mullins and Kayo, on the left, and Cap'n Midnite and Joyce are cartoon characters. These sets are made of chalkware, a poor wearing material prone to paint flaking. Both sets, $25.00-35.00.

UPPER CENTER: Goldilocks and bear made by Regal China Company. This set has a matching Cookie jar. Regal made an Alice in Wonderland set, and Old McDonald set consisting of many pieces, $45.00-55.00. Dick Tracy and Junior, in excellent condition for chalkware, $25.00-35.00.

LOWER CENTER: Peanuts as chef and Woodstock, $10.00-15.00. Betty Boop serenading her dog in a wooden boat, $15.00-20.00. This set is new—Vandor.

BOTTOM: These look like cartoon characters but I'm not sure who they are. They might be from Toonerville Trolly, $10.00-12.00. These glass Moon Mullens (?) were also candy containers. Their hats are plastic, $8.00-10.00. Al Capp originated the *Shmoo* in his Li'l Abner strip, $12.00-15.00.

TOP LEFT: Paddington Bear, $12.00-15.00. Garfield the Cat, $12.00-15.00.

TOP RIGHT: The hare and the tortoise, $8.00-10.00. Red Riding Hood and the Wolf. There are many different sets of these. This set was unmarked, probably Japanese, $18.00-22.00.

CENTER: Aladdin and his magic lamp, $15.00-18.00. King Midas and his bag of gold, $15.00-18.00.

BOTTOM: Paul Bunyan and his blue ox Babe. There are several Paul Bunyan sets, one with a stump, but this is the nicest, $15.00-18.00. Tom Sawyer and Huck Finn, this a beautifully detailed set, $18.00-22.00.

TOP: A barber and pig, $8.00-12.00. Marcia Smith, a West coast collector, tracked down the origin of this one for me. Here's the poem:

"Barber, barber, shave a pig
How many hours will make a wig?
Four and twenty, that's enough
Give the barber a pinch of snuff."

(from an old nursery rhyme book).
Dwarf and toadstool house, $6.00-8.00.

UPPER CENTER: Two sets of Raggedy Ann and Andy dolls, not very old but delightful, $10.00-15.00.

LOWER CENTER: Two sets from Beatrix Pottery, Benjamin Bunny on the left, and Samuel Whiskers on the right. These are not marked, so are probably Japanese spinoffs and not the authentic Beatrix Potter made in England set, $10.00-12.00.

BOTTOM: Three versions of the Goose that Laid the Golden Egg: small china set, $6.00-8.00. Larger set, $7.00-9.00. Plastic set with eggs concealed inside, $8.00-12.00.

TOP LEFT: Another photo of Red Riding Hood made by Hull China Co. This shows the mustard pot which sells for more than the much larger cookie jar. The shakers and cookie jars are available. The other pieces are much more scarce.

TOP RIGHT: Two versions of Noah's Ark. The first depicting Noah, $10.00-15.00. The set on the right is far more detailed. The ark is a sugar bowl, half the top lifts off and is the lid, and contains a spoon. Pairs of animals attached are the salt and pepper shakers, $18.00-20.00.

CENTER: Heckle and Jeckle, $10.00-15.00.

BOTTOM LEFT: Smokey the Bear, two different versions, $8.00-12.00.

BOTTOM RIGHT: Children riding swans. These must be from an old fairy tale, but hours spent in the children's library revealed nothing, $8.00-12.00.

TOP LEFT: **Mermaids, sheer fantasy and delightful, $8.00-10.00.**

TOP RIGHT: **Toys. A drum and horn with a cannon, $5.00-7.00. Toy soldiers, $6.00-8.00.**

CENTER: **Yarn type dolls, $6.00-8.00. Chalkware jack in the box, $5.00-7.00.**

BOTTOM: **One piece duck, $8.00-10.00. Blocks and ball, $8.00-10.00. I sent this set to my son and daughter-in-law when my first grandchild was born.**

Fish & other Creatures
from the Sea

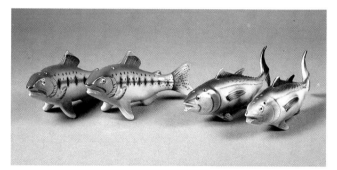

TOP: These are transition sets, fish or fantasy. $8.00-10.00.

UPPER CENTER LEFT: Fish nodders, $15.00-20.00. Turtles, $6.00-8.00.

UPPER CENTER RIGHT: These fish on the left look mean, $6.00-8.00.

LOWER CENTER LEFT: Fish, 5.00-7.00. I don't know how these birds got into this section; they're in a metal cage, $6.00-8.00.

LOWER CENTER RIGHT: Bright orange fish, $6.00-8.00. Red and white stylized fish, $5.00-7.00.

BOTTOM: Trout, vertical and horizontal, $8.00-10.00.

TOP LEFT: Swordfish, $6.00-8.00. Pink fish in wave base, $7.00-9.00.

TOP RIGHT: These might be big mouth bass, but they're not very realistic, $6.00-8.00. Turtles, $3.00-5.00.

UPPER CENTER: These have nice detail, $6.00-8.00. These 1920's looking ladies riding on fish are wonderful; the colors exactly match "Fiesta" pottery, and they are pure whimsy, $10.00-12.00.

LOWER CENTER: More "Fiesta" colored fish, $8.00-10.00. Fish sporting top hats, $6.00-8.00.

BOTTOM: Whales on a beach ball, $6.00-8.00. Puff fish, $5.00-7.00.

TOP LEFT: Laughing whales, $6.00-8.00. Bone china blue fish, $6.00-8.00.

TOP RIGHT: Whales with moveable eyes, $6.00-8.00. Sleek looking black and white whales from Nantucket, $6.00-8.00.

UPPER CENTER: Lobsters, $3.00-5.00. Sea horses, $6.00-8.00.

LOWER CENTER: Cartoon type octopus, $7.00-9.00. Ceramic Art Studio sea horse and coral, $18.00-22.00.

BOTTOM: These lobsters with springs on their claws are unusual, $8.00-10.00.

TOP: Two sizes of clam shells; the tiny ones are very realistic, $6.00-9.00.

CENTER LEFT: Star fish and shells, $6.00-8.00.

CENTER RIGHT: Whelk and Cowrie shells, $6.00-8.00.

BOTTOM: Deep sea divers, $8.00-10.00. Scallop shells, $6.00-8.00.

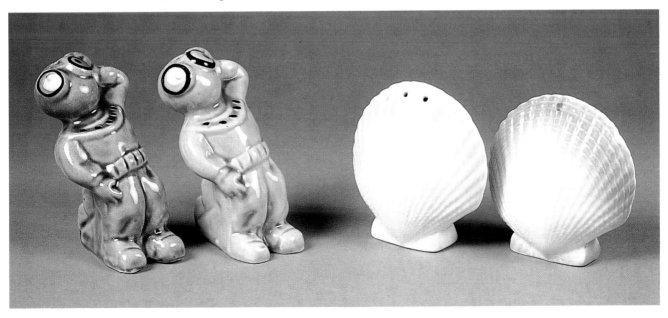

Food

TOP LEFT: A luscious basket of strawberries, good enough to eat, $8.00-10.00. Bananas, $6.00-8.00.

TOP RIGHT: These could also be called "go-withs"; turkey and roaster, $6.00-9.00. Bread in basket and cheese and apple on board, $8.00-10.00.

CENTER: Two baskets of fruit. In each, two pieces are removable and are the salt and pepper shakers, $8.00-10.00.

BOTTOM LEFT: Ham in frying pan, $8.00-10.00. Pancakes and syrup, $8.00-10.00.

BOTTOM RIGHT: Blackbird and pie, $6.00-8.00. Pig and roaster, $6.00-8.00.

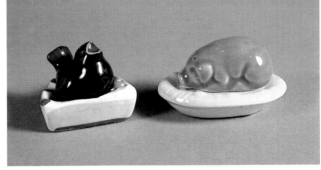

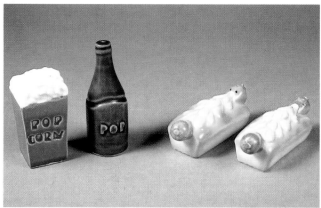

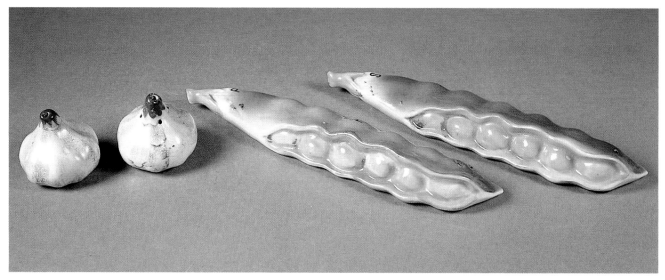

TOP LEFT: **Slices of pineapple. These are unusual, $8.00-10.00. Pie-a-la mode. The scoop of ice cream is the "pepper,"** $8.00-10.00.

TOP RIGHT: **Pop corn and soda, $8.00-10.00. Hot dogs in a roll. Note eyes, they look a little frightened at being buried in mustard, $8.00-10.00.**

CENTER: **Garlic, $6.00-8.00. Peas in a pod, $8.00-10.00.**

BOTTOM: **Ice cream sundae, $8.00-10.00. Straws and ice cream soda, $8.00-10.00.**

TOP: **Heads of lettuce in two sizes, large and small, $6.00-8.00.**

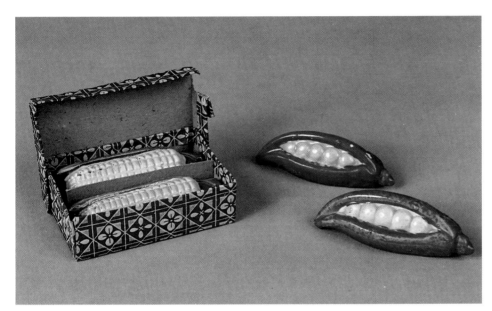

CENTER: **Corn in original box; a great box! $8.00-10.00. Small peas in pod, $6.00-8.00.**

BOTTOM: **Pumpkins all cut up for Halloween, $8.00-10.00.**

TOP: Grapes, $6.00-8.00. Pumpkins, $6.00-8.00.

CENTER: In these three sets, the branch is one shaker and the fruit is the other, $8.00-10.00.

BOTTOM: Chalkware, corn, $3.00-5.00. Baked potates with pat of butter, $6.00-8.00.

TOP: Saltines, these are so realistic looking, $8.00-10.00.

CENTER LEFT: There are so many different sets of corn shakers. This one is upright, $6.00-8.00 pr. Very large celery, $6.00-8.00.

CENTER RIGHT: This set of pumpkin and gourd was put out by Avon, $6.00-8.00.

BOTTOM: This is a most unusual selection. At least I have never seen these before. Real cans (I had to open them with a can opener to have them photographed) with vegetables inside. The cans are tin; the shakers ceramic, $12.00-15.00.

TOP: **Metal stand with glass ice cream cones (metal tops), $8.00-10.00. This set is luster ware; a dog pushing an ice cream cart that says "stop me and buy one"; the lids of the shakers say "ICE" and "CREAM," $15.00-18.00.**

This could almost be considered a separate category and highly collectible - Fruit and Vegetable People.

CENTER: **Onion people taking it easy, $8.00-10.00. Apple heads, $8.00-10.00.**

BOTTOM LEFT: **Pineapple people, $8.00-10.00. These fruit people really look like people, $10.00-12.00.**

BOTTOM RIGHT: **Peach head, $6.00-8.00. Grape people, $8.00-10.00.**

TOP: Corn. These just have eyes and nose; not as interesting, $6.00-8.00. The banana heads have bodies underneath. These are great, $8.00-10.00.

CENTER: This pair is most unusual; the people have vegetable heads, but their bodies are far more detailed than usual, $12.00-15.00. Beet people, $8.00-10.00.

BOTTOM: Creamer and sugar head people (to go with the fork and spoon and the dishes and pots and pans), $8.00-10.00. Celery and carrot people. They look like they're saying "don't eat me!" $8.00-10.00.

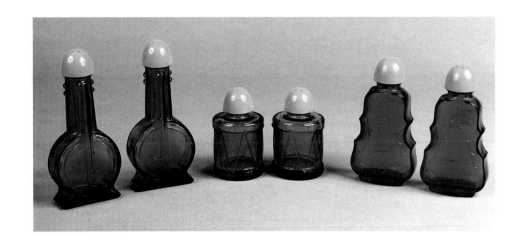

Glass, Metal and Wood

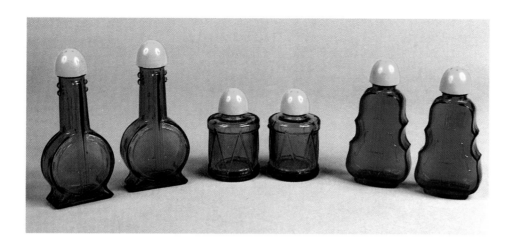

TOP: Cobalt glass shakers with yellow plastic tops. Since this photograph was taken, I found another pair in the series, accordians. I would be curious to know if there are other, $12.00-15.00.

CENTER: These birds are Czechoslovakian. The heads are china and screw on. These are chickens and ducks; I have also seen them with orange heads, $22.00-25.00.

BOTTOM: These glass dogs and cats have metal heads. The glass is pink and green as in Depression glass, and the heads are silver plated. They may have originally been candy containers, $35.00-50.00.

TOP LEFT: Glass shakers with bakelite tops. There are many varieties of these, some with metal and some with glass trays, $6.00-9.00.

TOP RIGHT: These miniature bottles have plastic tops and are not very old, $3.00-5.00.

UPPER CENTER: There are many black and white metal sets with Amish-type decoration. The most common ones are household objects. Bean pots and gramaphones, $6.00-8.00.

LOWER CENTER: Two types of coffee grinders, $6.00-8.00.

BOTTOM: The clowns and the dog in the shoe are less common, $8.00-10.00. Butter churns, $6.00-8.00.

TOP LEFT: These are the kind that are great for dollhouses. Stoves, rocking chairs and wringer washers, $6.00-8.00.

TOP RIGHT: Wells and sewing machines, $6.00-8.00.

UPPER CENTER: This metal pair is from Siam; it is brass with toothpick holder, $7.00-9.00. Radiators, $6.00-8.00.

LOWER CENTER: Paint tubes, gold and silver. These are so realistic the tendency is to pick them up and squeeze them, $18.00-24.00. Old fashioned telephones, $6.00-8.00.

BOTTOM: Silver color ducks. Occupied Japan, $12.00-15.00. Squirrel, $8.00-10.00. Owls with glass eyes, $10.00-12.00.

TOP LEFT: These metal shakers look like cocktail shakers, $8.00-10.00. The chrome boat is a wonderful deco piece. The smokestack tops are bakelite, and it has a small compartment for mustard, $18.00-24.00.

TOP RIGHT: These two sets were made by the Chase Brass and Copper Company, Waterbury, Connecticut. These are chrome plated. The company made many pieces of Art Deco design in the 1930's. Spheres, larger one is salt, $15.00-20.00. Cubes with Saturn and a comet are much less common. They have an ivory bakelite insert, $22.00-28.00.

CENTER: This brass bellhop holds two glass shakers, $15.00-18.00.

BOTTOM LEFT: This lamp with salt and pepper may have been used in a restaurant. The batteries inside were marked 29¢, $15.00-18.00. Brass colored hurricane lamp, $6.00-8.00.

BOTTOM RIGHT: Metal and glass umbrella holder, $8.00-10.00. Metal tea wagon with glass shakers, $8.00-10.00.

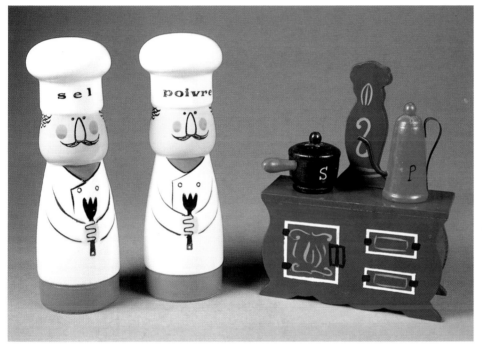

TOP: These three sets of cans are in plastic baskets. They are souvenir sets from the 1970's. The Prudential Center, Boston, MA, New Mexico, Corn Palace, Mitchell, SD, $8.00-10.00.

CENTER: French Chefs, $8.00-10.00. Wooden stove, pots on top are shakers, $8.00-10.00.

BOTTOM: A nice bright chicken and egg set, $6.00-8.00. Chefs, $6.00-8.00.

Miniatures

Most of the miniatures were made by Arcadia Ceramics, Inc. of Arcadia, California. They were made for collectors and were packed in a bubble pack. They are much too tiny to be of any use as a receptacle. They average 1½″ in height. The instructions say to cover hole with tape as they're too small to use a cork.

TOP LEFT: Drunk on park bench and lamp post, $8.00-10.00. Cannibal cooking white man in pot, $8.00-10.00.

TOP RIGHT: Typewriter and telephone. This is one of the most detailed sets I've seen. Note the cord on the telephone, $8.00-10.00. Birthday cake and slice. There are many variations of this, $8.00-10.00.

UPPER CENTER: Barn and hay wagon, $8.00-10.00. Scarecrow and corn stalks, $8.00-10.00.

LOWER CENTER: Turkey and covered roasting pan, $6.00-8.00. Soda and straws in holder (very similar to larger set), $8.00-10.00. Pie and rolling pin, $8.00-10.00.

BOTTOM: Gun in holster and cowboy hat, $8.00-10.00. Congratulations book and gift package, $8.00-10.00.

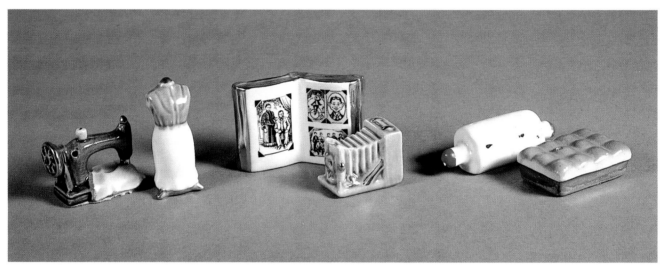

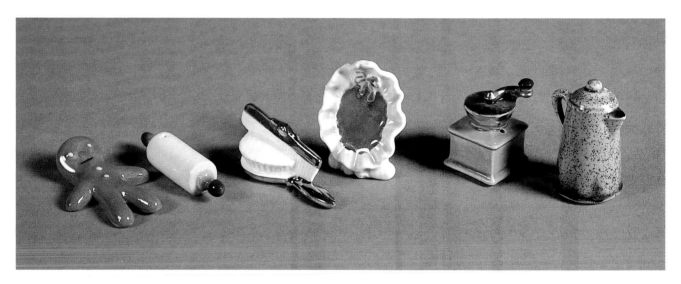

TOP LEFT: Swinging barroom door and spittoon, $6.00-8.00. Donkey and wagon full of grapes, $8.00-10.00.

TOP RIGHT: Fish in boat, will he hook the sailor? $8.00-10.00. Donut and cup of coffee, $6.00-8.00.

CENTER: Sewing machine and dress form-wonderful! 8.00-10.00. Photo album and camera, $8.00-10.00. Rolling pin and muffins, $6.00-8.00.

BOTTOM: Rolling pin and gingerbread man, $8.00-10.00. Comb and brush and mirror, $8.00-10.00. Coffee grinder and coffee pot, $8.00-10.00.

TOP: **Baby in carriage (does it go with bottle?) $3.00-5.00. Cradle and spinning wheel, $8.00-10.00.**

CENTER: **Bowling ball and pin, $8.00-10.00. Mitt with ball, cap and bat, $8.00-10.00.**

BOTTOM LEFT: **Key and lock, $6.00-8.00. These two people are from "Three men in a tub" the third man is attached to the tub. They aren't mine. Incomplete.**

BOTTOM RIGHT: **Fireplace and coal hod, $6.00-8.00.**

119

Nodders & Huggers

TOP: This wonderful nodder belongs to Irene Thornburg of Michigan, who was kind enough to send me this picture. The most common nodders are in a white rectangular base. The most desirable kind are the figural ones, and this is exceptional. Elephant with clown and dog, $40.00-50.00.

BOTTOM: This Irish set from Lake Killarney is nicely painted, $15.00-18.00.

TOP: Chickens in a typical rose decorated base, $15.00-18.00. Black cat figural base, both the large cat and small cat heads are the nodders, $22.00-25.00.

UPPER CENTER: Indians in a drum base, $18.00-24.00. Pennsylvania Dutch. "We get too soon old and too late smart." If anyone understands the significance of the four eyes on the man, I would be interested in hearing about it, $18.00-22.00.

LOWER CENTER LEFT: Flamingos and ducks in a similar base, $15.00-18.00.

LOWER CENTER RIGHT: Teddy bears and alligators. These are souvenir sets, $15.00-18.00.

BOTTOM: Another set from Ireland. The young couple are in a heart shaped base. The red lid covers a mustard pot, $22.00-25.00.

TOP: Monkeys in base, $16.00-18.00. The gray haired black woman is another rare set. Her head is the nodder. The watermelon is the other shaker, and when it's removed, she is bare-bosomed, $40.00-50.00. Another set with mustard pot. These horses and jockeys are nice, $18.00-22.00.

CENTER: Chickens, teddy bears and fish, $15.00-18.00.

BOTTOM: Deer, $15.00-18.00.

The following sets of shakers, called "huggers," were designed by Ruth van Tellingen Bendel. There are Japanese copies, but the originals are marked. Van Tellingen is impressed across the bottom of the back. Some say "Bunny Hugs" or "Bear Hugs."

TOP: **Mary and lamb, $20.00-24.00. Yellow Ducks, $12.00-14.00. Dutch boy and girl, $16.00-18.00.**

BOTTOM: **Sailor and Mermaid (more scarce than others), $22.00-26.00. Green love bugs, $12.00-14.00. Bunny hugs, these also come in white and pink, $10.00-14.00.**

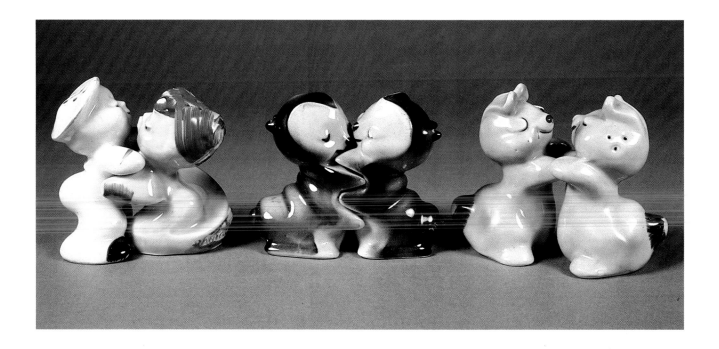

People—Occupations

TOP LEFT: These sets are quite comical. The holes for the salt and pepper are the eyes. Doctors with tools and shoemakers, $8.00-10.00.

TOP RIGHT: Nuns, $8.00-10.00. Friars, $6.00-8.00.

CENTER: Set of three friars on heart-shaped tray; salt, pepper and mustard. Made by Apco, $12.00-15.00.

BOTTOM: Heads with moveable glass eyes, made in Germany, $10.00-12.00. Small monk and friar, $8.00-10.00.

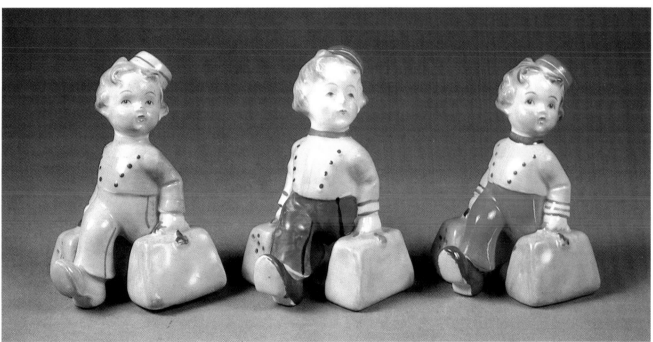

TOP: Bell hop. One piece shaker. Shake one way for salt. The other for pepper, $10.00-12.00. Redcap pushing cart. Two center suitcases remove and are the salt and pepper, $12.00-15.00.

BOTTOM: These three bellhops are identical except for color. They are also one piece shakers. The holes are in front of one suitcase, in back of the other. These are reminiscent of Johnny of *Philip Morris* fame. They are delightful, $12.00-15.00.

TOP LEFT: The Gloucester fisherman, souvenir of Cape Cod, $6.00-8.00. Captain and mate, chalkware, paint flaking, $4.00-6.00.

TOP RIGHT: Sailor boy and girl, sitting on a bench, $8.00-10.00. Seamens' heads, interesting detail, $6.00-8.00.

CENTER: A pair of "Old Salts," $6.00-8.00. Organ grinder and monkey. This is a particularly nice one, $15.00-18.00.

BOTTOM: Chefs with black cat and chicken, marked Shafford china, $10.00-12.00. This replica of the old G.E. refrigerator is pottery. It is labeled IDLEWILD, the former name of JFK Airport in N.Y. With chef, $10.00-12.00.

TOP: **Ever popular clowns. There are probably thousands of clown salt and pepper shakers out there. Clown on drum, $10.00-12.00. Dog on ball, dressed as clown. $8.00-10.00.**

CENTER: **American pottery clowns. These in unusually good condition, $8.00-10.00. Clown heads in tall hats, $8.00-10.00.**

BOTTOM: **Clown reamers. These clowns in two sizes have hats like reamers or juicers. Large, $12.00-15.00. Small, $10.00-12.00.**

TOP: **Both of these bellhops are holding suitcases that are the salt and pepper shakers. The larger set has holes in his hands for the handles, $12.00-15.00. The smaller set has curved hands and the suitcases slip on (and off), $12.00-15.00.**

CENTER: **Cowboys made in Czechoslovakia, $8.00-10.00. Bear and hunter, $6.00-8.00.**

BOTTOM: **The little boy cowboy and his lying down horse are quite charming, $10.00-12.00. Cowboy and standing horse, $8.00-10.00. This looks like the same cowboy whose hat comes off and is a separate shaker, but it's not. This cowboy and his hat are attached. The other shaker is the stagecoach, $8.00-10.00.**

130

TOP: Beermeister with three barrels. One is mustard pot, $12.00-15.00.

CENTER: Deep sea diver and treasure chest, $8.00-10.00. Pirate and treasure chest, $8.00-10.00.

BOTTOM: Little boy dressed up as pirate with treasure chest, $8.00-10.00. A pair of clowns marked Glee and Glum, $10.00-15.00.

TOP: The next four sets are part of the same series. I would be interested in hearing from anyone who has seen others in the series or who might know anything about them. Driver in green car, $10.00-12.00. Sailor in lavender boat, $10.00-12.00.

BOTTOM: Chef with rolling pin, $10.00-12.00. Fireman with red (what else?) fire engine, $10.00-12.00.

TOP: Firemen hats. These are quite large, and of pottery, $8.00-10.00. Mexican "Charros." The Sunday cowboys seen in Chapultepec Park in Mexico City, $8.00-10.00.

CENTER: Railroad workers. These must be sold at souvenir shops at various sites, Steamtown, U.S.A. Bellows Falls, VT, $10.00-12.00.

BOTTOM: More R.R. workers. These from Strasburg, Pa, $10.00-12.00. A lone Royal Canadian Mounted Police "sans" horse, $5.00. A butler and maid. I believe someone painted the names on them afterwards. These have a "1940's" look, $10.00-12.00.

TOP: There are many varieties of the RCMP's. Many are mounted on a horse, and each is a shaker. The pair on the right, however, is standing. These look more like figurines than salt and pepper shakers, $12.00-15.00.

CENTER: Doctor and nurse (when will they begin to make women Doctors?), $8.00-10.00. Island police. These look like Bahamian or Caribbean, $8.00-10.00.

BOTTOM: Toy soldiers, $6.00-8.00. British bobby and palace guard, $8.00-10.00.

TOP: Mailman and woman, $8.00-10.00. These came out in 1968 and were distributed by Heather House, Burlington, Iowa. Apparently they heard my question. They came out with three city employees. Each set consisted of a man and woman in uniform, and they sold for $1.25 a set. Still no female doctor! Fireman, $8.00-10.00.

CENTER: Policeman couple from the same municipal series, $8.00-10.00. Baseball players from Cooperstown, NY Baseball Hall of Fame, $8.00-10.00.

BOTTOM: Cartoon type police with billy clubs, $6.00-8.00. Drunk and lamp post, New Orleans, LA, $6.00-8.00.

135

TOP LEFT: Boxers, including black eye, good when serving beef steak, $10.00-12.00.

TOP RIGHT: Golf ball and tee, $6.00-8.00. Canadian hockey players (unusual), $10.00-12.00.

CENTER: There are six sets of these sports figures pictured here. Again, I wonder if anyone has seen others. Football, boxing, bowling, $8.00-12.00.

BOTTOM: Baseball, golf, skiing, $8.00-12.00.

TOP: Devils, chalkware, $5.00-7.00. Angel and Devil, $6.00-8.00.

BOTTOM: A large single devil. I don't know what goes with it, $4.00-5.00. Skeleton or ghost shakers marked poison. There is a liquor decanter that matches these, $8.00-10.00.

People—Nationalities

TOP: American Pilgrims. These were put out by Hallmark in 1970 for Thanksgiving, $8.00-10.00. Dutch couple, made by Goebel (German), $20.00-25.00.

CENTER: Oriental couple. These are made by Ceramic Arts Studio in Wisconsin and come in two sizes. This is the smaller, $18.00-22.00. The Dutch couple is also Ceramic Arts Studio. Their faces have a very characteristic look. They are clearly marked, and so readily identifiable, $18.00-22.00.

BOTTOM: Oriental couple on base with pagoda, $10.00-12.00. Eastern native on elephant, $12.00-15.00. German made elves (?) with crows. I thought these might represent a folk tale, but I have been unable to find out anything about them. Help would be most welcome, $12.00-15.00.

TOP LEFT: Oriental couple, $6.00-8.00. Red and black seated couple, $6.00-8.00.

CENTER: Oriental with rickshaw, $8.00-10.00. Couple, $6.00-8.00.

TOP RIGHT: Confucious with sign, $8.00-10.00. Oriental heads, $6.00-8.00.

BOTTOM: These fat figures are different and very charming, $8.00-10.00.

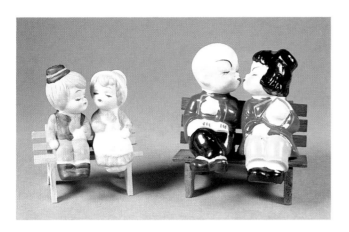

TOP LEFT: Irish couple on bench, $8.00-10.00. Oriental couple on bench, $8.00-10.00.
TOP RIGHT: Dutch couple on bench, $8.00-10.00. Eskimo couple on bench, $8.00-10.00.
CENTER: Dutch couple. Made in Germany, these are finely detailed, $10.00-12.00. Windmill, $6.00-8.00 (pr.)
BOTTOM LEFT: Scotch couple kissing, $8.00-10.00. These look like they represent Thailand or Siam, $8.00-10.00.
BOTTOM RIGHT: These look like English story book characters, $5.00-7.00.

People—General

TOP: Hummel-type children. These are Japanese copies and very nicely done. Many sets exist, $12.00-15.00.

CENTER LEFT: Graduates. These are similar to the series of the couples who are the city workers, $8.00-10.00.

CENTER RIGHT: These certainly look like a pair, but I don't see the connection. The boy looks like a construction worker, and the girl like a maid. They're both "pretty," $6.00-8.00.

BOTTOM: Amish couple, ceramic, $6.00-8.00. Amish type horse and wagon, $6.00-8.00.

TOP LEFT: Weird couple on a bench, $8.00-10.00. Weird couple, $6.00-8.00.

TOP RIGHT: More strange looking people. The taller pair are "peppy pa and salty ma." The small pair have glittery eyes, $6.00-8.00.

CENTER: Grandma and Grandpa on rockers, $8.00-10.00. This girl selling fruit is lovely and older than most, probably pre-World War II, $10.00-12.00.

BOTTOM: Dinosaurs, $8.00-10.00. Cave man and woman, $8.00-10.00.

TOP LEFT: Two sweet old fashioned girls in yellow, $6.00-8.00. A charming couple, similar to the Hummel type, but these are all dressed in white and gold, $10.00-12.00.

TOP RIGHT: Another attractive couple. These look like 1960's, $8.00-10.00. Heads of girls, $5.00-7.00.

CENTER: More child-couples, $5.00-7.00.

BOTTOM: This set is rather charming. The tiny people holding flowers fit into a neat little holder, $8.00-10.00. Stylized bell hops bringing flowers, $6.00-8.00.

TOP LEFT: These four girls were made by NAPCO (National Pottery Co.) They represent different months, the yellow, April, the green and lavender, May and the orange, August, $8.00-10.00 pr.

TOP RIGHT: Revolutionary war soldiers, $8.00-10.00. Copies of Staffordshire men. These are from Staffordshire, but they are not old. (English), $15.00-18.00.

CENTER LEFT: Kewpies. The smaller pair are shiny china, $8.00-10.00. The larger kewpies are bisque and shedding tears, $10.00-12.00.

CENTER RIGHT: Hoboes, $5.00-7.00. Grandpa and Grandma without their rockers, $6.00-8.00.

BOTTOM: These are among my favorites (as are so many). Art deco shape and style, these people are of Japanese luster, $15.00-18.00.

TOP: This delightful couple have one arm in front and the other around each other in the back. A bit of whimsy, $10.00-12.00. Still no pair for the "taxi lady." The small round fat shaker is also luster ware, $6.00-8.00 ea.

CENTER: Bride and groom. There are an endless variety of these. My son and his wife used a Goebel pair I had given them on their wedding cake. $10.00-12.00. This pair is not only unusual, but very intricate. The groom is carrying the bride over the threshold. Remember those days? $15.00-18.00.

BOTTOM: Another bride and groom. This groom in a dark suit, $8.00-10.00. A tiny figurine type couple in fancy dress, very elegant, $8.00-10.00.

147

TOP: Bride and groom in 1950's type car. She has a real bit of veil on, and the car has space for mustard, $10.00-12.00. This maid, carrying two shakers in the shape of eggs, is beautiful porcelain. I saw it in an antique shop in England for $50.00. When I asked the dealer why it was so "pricey," he explained that it had been on the cover of a magazine called *Working Women* in the 1930's, $25.00-40.00.

CENTER and BOTTOM: Another 2-sided figure. A bride and groom marked "love and marriage" on one side, with the bride questioning. On the other side, the wife has a baby, and the husband is questioning marriage; notice he's carrying the bottle! $12.00-15.00.

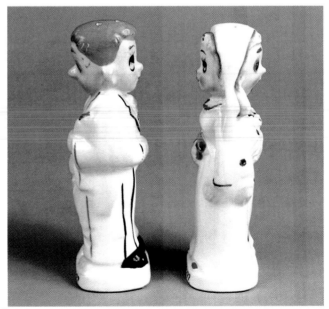

148

TOP: Another couple with a baby. They both look exhausted, but the baby looks great, $8.00-10.00.

CENTER: Here an old maid is praying for a man, and there's one right under her bed, $8.00-10.00. This is an older couple, written across her skirt says "you and your once more for old times' sake. He just looks perplexed. This is a fun gift for a second or older marriage. A friend of mine gave it as a shower gift, and it made a big hit, $8.00-10.00.

BOTTOM: Two pairs of little people, $6.00-8.00.

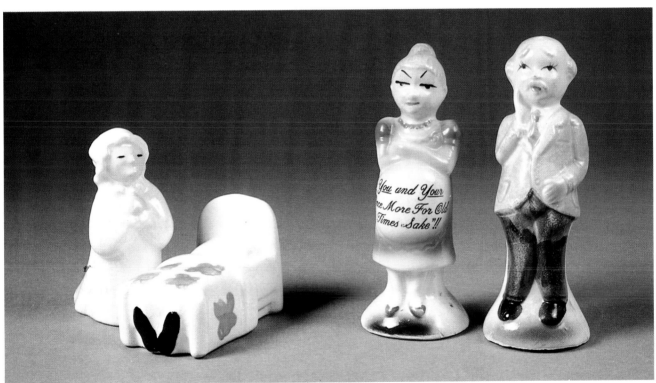

TOP and CENTER: These two couples are two part shakers. The boy's top hat comes off and is the separate shaker. The girl's head comes off and is the separate shaker. I'd rather be the boy, $10.00-12.00.

BOTTOM: A pair of girls and their poodle. These look like Barbie dolls and are probably from the 1960's, $10.00-12.00. A pair of bathing beauties. These look more like 1940's, $12.00-15.00.

TOP: Heads, farmer and wife, $6.00-8.00. Really ugly toby type mugs, $6.00-8.00.

CENTER: Chef heads, $6.00-8.00. Drip and Drop (these come in several colors), $6.00-8.00.

BOTTOM: These heads are very nicely detailed. They look like an English literary character, but I'm not sure, $8.00-10.00. A couple of laughing heads, $6.00-8.00.

TOP: Kissing couple. These are very charming, $8.00-10.00.

BOTTOM: More kissing couples. The couple with the pointed hat, their arms painted on each other. If you look closely you can see a pink arm on the man and a white arm on the woman, $12.00-15.00. This couple looks Eastern Mediterranean, $6.00-8.00.

TOP: Children in bunny outfits, $8.00-10.00. Dutch kissing couple, $8.00-10.00.

CENTER: Hillbilly with two jugs (hard plastic), $5.00-7.00. Dutch boy with water buckets, $6.00-8.00.

BOTTOM: Grandmother and Grandfather on rockers. This is two pairs. The rockers are also shakers, $8.00-10.00.

People—Risque'

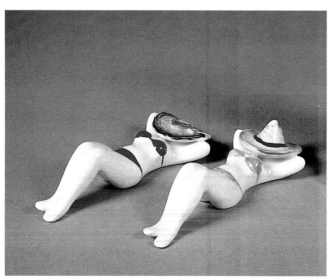

(These were also called "naughties")

TOP: **Sailor and Mermaid, $12.00-15.00. Girl on alligator, $15.00-15.00.**

CENTER: **Man and woman in fancy dress, $15.00-18.00.**

BOTTOM: **Same man and woman from the rear, $15.00-18.00.**

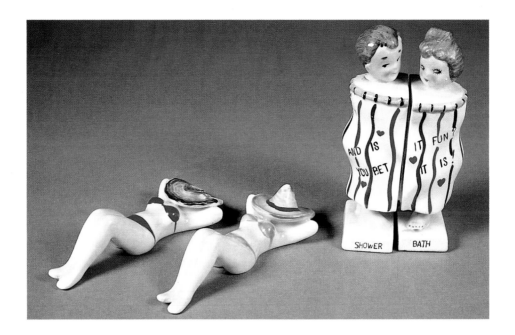

TOP: A pair of bikini clad girls sunbathing, $10.00-12.00. A couple taking a shower says "is it fun? You bet it is!", $12.00-15.00.

CENTER LEFT: A torso split in half, a bit morbid for the dinner table! $10.00-12.00. Bisque nudes (a la Gauguin), $8.00-10.00.

CENTER RIGHT: Nudes decorating barrels. The larger ones are wearing pearls, small, $6.00-8.00, larger pair, $8.00-10.00.

BOTTOM: The upright nudes are just a torso, $8.00-10.00. Lying down nudes, two out of three have no heads! $8.00-10.00. I recently saw a pair of these in a souvenir shop on the Boardwalk in Atlantic City. (Yes, I look for salt and pepper shakers everywhere!) These were new and of much lighter weight pottery than the old ones pictured here. When I asked to see them, the clerk said "Oh, you mean the Dolly Parton ones!"

People & Places—Historic

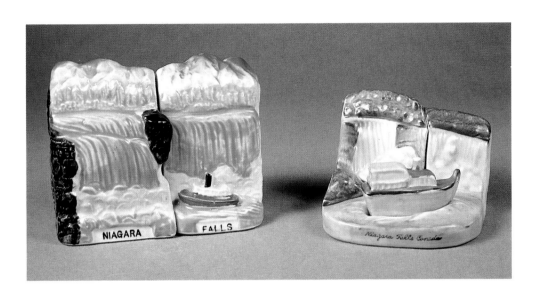

LEFT: Pricilla and John Alden, $8.00-10.00.

TOP RIGHT: Small metal pilgrims, $8.00-10.00. Pricilla and John, $8.00-10.00.

CENTER & BOTTOM: These historic sets from the 1950's have a bust of a famous figure paired with a scroll giving biographical data. These were sold through the Heather House catalog in 1967 and were $1.00 pr. or 6 prs. for $5.00. Will Rogers and Christopher Columbus were also included in this set. They were made by Parkcraft, the same company that made the states, the months and the cities. Christopher Columbus, Will Rogers, Betsy Ross, Geo. Washington, Benj Franklin, Chas. Lindbergh Buffalo Bill, $15.00-18.00 per pair.

TOP: Eisenhower lock, St. Lawrence Seaway, $15.00-18.00. Bust of General Eisenhower. Head and torso are separate shakers. Bottom says "We like Ike," $22.00-25.00.

CENTER: The Carter smile on ceramic peanuts, $10.00-12.00. Plains, Ga. Home of Jimmy Carter, $6.00-8.00.

BOTTOM: The presidents carved on Mt. Rushmore, brown and white china, $8.00-10.00. (These also come in a silver colored metal.)

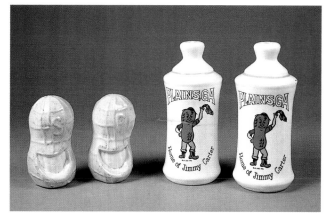

TOP: Cylinders with decals of presidents, all have the same base, Truman, Eisenhower, Cleveland, Roosevelt and Jefferson, $6.00-8.00.

CENTER: Another shaped cylinder: Robert and John Kennedy; Nixon, $6.00-8.00.

BOTTOM: These bases trimmed in gold generally had the president and his wife. The Johnson's and the Kennedy's, $6.00-8.00.

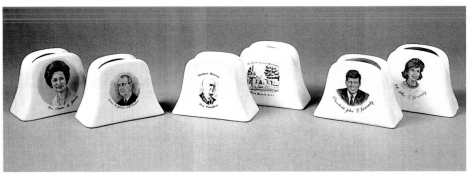

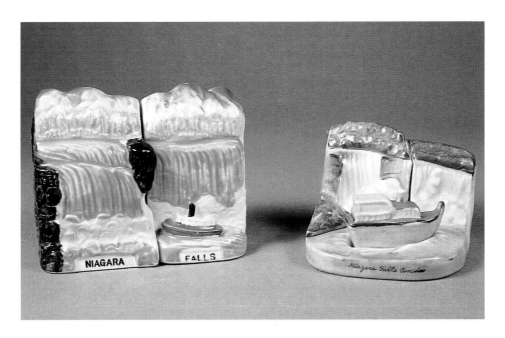

TOP: Two versions of Niagara Falls; one splits and each half is the salt and pepper, $8.00-10.00. The second set has the boat, Maid of the Mist, as one shaker, and half the falls as the other, $8.00-10.00.

CENTER LEFT: Plymouth Rock marked 1620, $6.00-8.00. The Mayflower and Plymouth Rock, $8.00-10.00.

CENTER RIGHT: Santa's Workshop, North Pole, N.Y. (not exactly historic), $8.00-10.00. The House of Seven Gables, Salem, Mass, $6.00-8.00.

BOTTOM: Hersheypark, Hershey, Pa, $8.00-10.00. 1939 World's Fair, N.Y. Trylon and perisphere, ceramic on tray, $20.00-25.00.

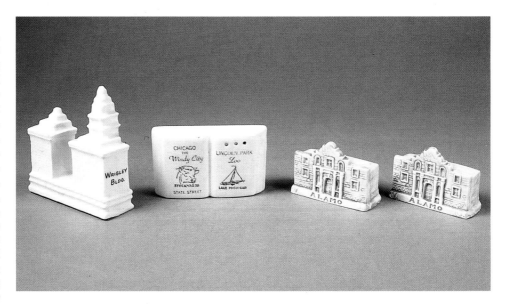

TOP: Wrigley Building, Chicago with book depicting famous sites; part of a series also sold through Heather House made by Parkcraft. Set includes London, Paris, Tokyo, Killarney, Philadelphia, Capetown Toronto, Havana, Agra, Amsterdam, Washington, Venice, Cairo, Rio de Janeiro, Honolulu, Hannibal & Springfield. Each set consisted of a symbol and book of the city. In 1967, they were selling for 55¢ a pair! (6 prs for 3.00), $15.00-18.00. The Alamo, $5.00-7.00.

CENTER: 1968 World's Fair, San Antonio, Texas, $8.00-10.00. Plastic snow-shaker salt and pepper of Washington, D.C. The front of these is filled with water and "snow"; the back has the chamber for salt and pepper, $10.00-12.00.

BOTTOM LEFT: Kennedy Space Center, Florida, ceramic, $10.00-12.00. Seattle Space Needle, metal, $8.00-10.00.

BOTTOM RIGHT: 1939 World's Fair, plastic push button set all in one, $12.00-15.00. Trylon and Perisphere in heavy silver pot metal, $12.00-15.00.

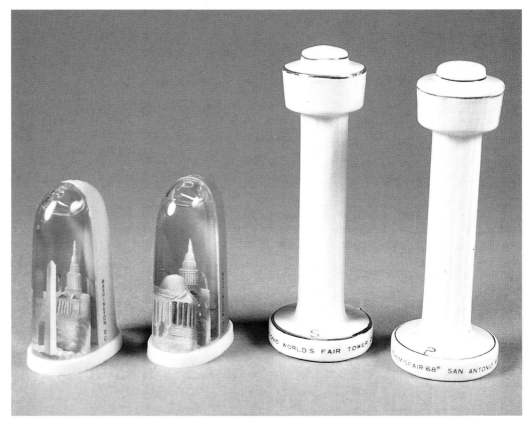

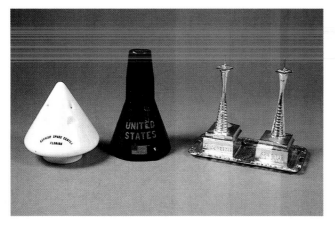

TOP: **Pot metal, Washington Monument, $8.00-10.00. Castle from Disneyland, $10.00-12.00.**

CENTER: **Bok Tower, Florida, $8.00-10.00. Utah, shape of state, 2 identical, $6.00-8.00.**

BOTTOM: **Two sets of Washington, D.C. on rose decorated metal tray, $15.00-18.00.**

TOP: Statue of Liberty and Empire State Building on tray, N.Y.C., $15.00-18.00. Little America, Wyoming, $8.00-10.00.

CENTER: I bought this Statue of Liberty set in New York City during Liberty Weekend, July 4, 1986, the celebration of the Statue's 100th birthday. They cost $15.00, but I haven't seen them around since, $15.00-18.00. Sea Gulls, same vintage, $12.00-15.00.

BOTTOM: Lions International, $8.00-10.00. Horse shoe and four leaf clover from McCann's store, Torrington, Ct. Printed on back of horse shoe is "Lucky 75th Anniversary, 1950." $10.00-12.00.

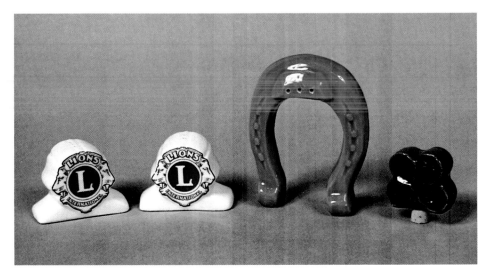

Plastic

TOP: Orange frying pans. These are like the silver and copper color Revere type set, but less common, $8.00-10.00. White TV. Most of these that I've seen have been brown, $10.00-12.00.

CENTER: White toaster. The chrome colored one is much more common, $10.00-15.00. Fried eggs. The yolks are the shakers, $10.00-12.00.

BOTTOM: Bakelite, early plastic, developed by Dr. L.H. Bakeland in the U.S. in 1909. It was primarily an industrial material and is characterized by an opaque and often marbelized appearance and in muted colors of green, yellow-orange, black, and bright red. The shapes of bakelite shakers were usually very geometric and often deco. These two pairs are representative of the genre, $22.00-28.00.

TOP: Bakelite shakers. The palm tree stand is regular plastic, $20.00-22.00.

CENTER: Wonderful color, wonderful shape, $8.00-10.00.

BOTTOM: An English woman I met gave me the bakelite condiment set on tray. This is the typical butterscotch color. She said that in England during World War II goods were so scarce that this was something she received for a wedding present - from an affluent friend, $20.00-25.00. These penguins are bakelite, and I found them in a flea market in London; ivory is the other common color of bakelite, $20.00-25.00.

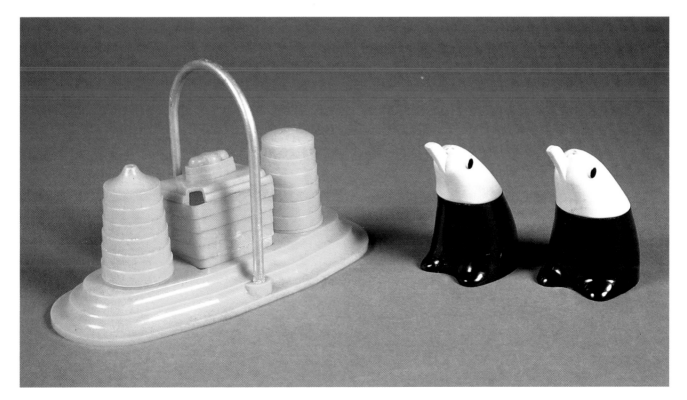

TOP: This rotisserie is the only one I've seen. Plastic chickens on a spit inside are the salt and pepper shakers. The clear plastic front opens; all the dials and controls are depicted. This set is extremely realistic, $15.00-18.00. Chrome-looking coffee maker in original box, $8.00-12.00.

CENTER: Irons, all of the chrome colored appliances are very realistic, $8.00-10.00. Sewing machine, the top opens and closes like a real treadle sewing machine. The drawers are the salt and pepper, $10.00-12.00.

BOTTOM: Lanterns, $6.00-8.00. This is the only mixmaster I have seen with a clear, rather than opaque white bowl and beaters. The beaters are the salt and pepper, and the bowl is for sugar, $15.00-18.00.

TOP: Black and white clothespin with faces, $6.00-8.00. Pump, the salt and pepper come up out of the top when the lever is pushed up and down. The bucket is for sugar, $10.00-12.00.

CENTER: Fireplace with andirons. The andirons are the shakers, $8.00-10.00. Piano. The common one is white with gold. This green and red one is for Christmas and even has Christmas Carols on the music stand, $10.00-12.00.

BOTTOM: Orange tree with baskets as salt and pepper, $10.00-12.00. Basket of fruit. Center pineapple and grapefruit come out and are the salt and pepper. The base is for sugar, $8.00-10.00.

169

TOP: This may take the prize for the ugliest shaker! Onion people shakers on a cart made up of vegetables, carrots, celery, etc., $6.00-8.00.

CENTER: Mirror hat stand; this is much harder to find than the hat rack that has the same two hats as salt and pepper shaker; that one is a stand with toothpick holder at base, $12.00-15.00.

BOTTOM: Roller skates, $8.00-10.00. Golf balls on green, $10.00-12.00.

TOP: Scale, $8.00-10.00. Paint palette with two glass jars; plastic tops, $10.00-12.00.

CENTER: Snow shakers. These look like television sets. The chamber for salt and pepper is on the side. The middle is filled with water and snow (according to Nancy McMichael, snow dome collector, par excellence, the snow is shaved paraffin and mothballs). From left to right: Civic Center, Los Angeles, Canada and Grauman's Chinese, Hollywood, $10.00-15.00.

BOTTOM: More snow shakers. These have the salt and pepper in the opaque section in the back, $8.00-10.00.

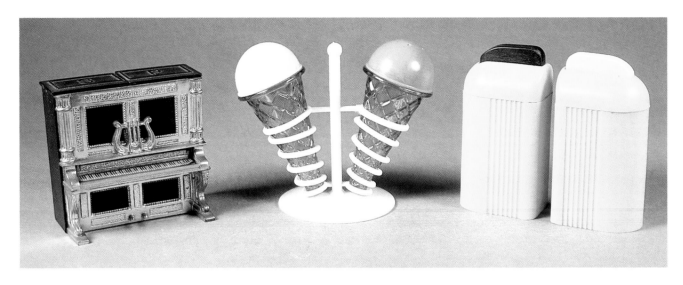

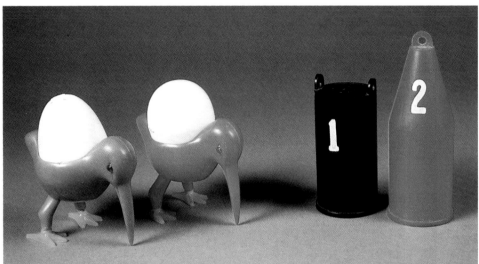

TOP: Black and gold piano, $10.00-12.00. Glass ice cream cones in plastic stand with plastic tops, $8.00-10.00. Tall push button set for use on stove, $6.00-8.00.

CENTER: Great looking birds with egg shakers, $8.00-10.00. These are English Channel markers; the black one is called a can and the red one is called a Nun. They are from 1940. $8.00-10.00.

BOTTOM: Wooden look plastic ice boxes, $5.00-7.00. Kitchen witches, $5.00-7.00. Clocks, $5.00-7.00.

TOP: **Red Humpty Dumpty, $5.00-7.00.**

CENTER: **Tomato and pepper, $5.00-7.00. Two in one shaker, $4.00-6.00.**

BOTTOM: **Yellow birdcage, $6.00-7.00. Hanging apple, $3.00-5.00.**

TOP LEFT: **Kitchen set with chef, $3.00-5.00. Toaster from Arizona, $6.00-8.00.**

TOP RIGHT: **Chefs under awning, $5.00-7.00. Chef holding shakers, $6.00-8.00.**

CENTER: **Tiny Dutch couple, $3.00-5.00. Dutch girl with glass bottles. These may have been candy containers, $6.00-8.00.**

BOTTOM: **Two monkeys hanging from a branch, $3.00-5.00. Ships, shakers are the smokestacks, $5.00-7.00.**

174

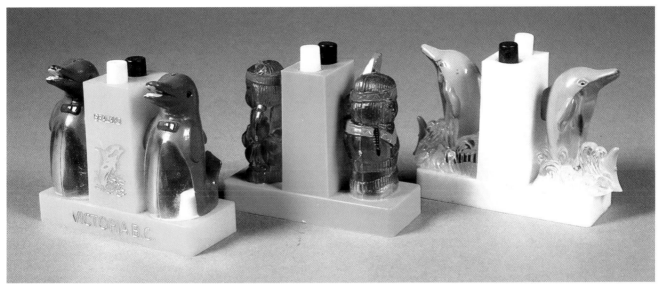

TOP: **One piece push button shakers: Pigs, blacks, Amish and alligators, $4.00-6.00.**

CENTER: **Penguins, Indians and porpoises, $4.00-6.00.**

BOTTOM: Lucite with rose embedded in center, $3.00-5.00. Glass in bakelite tray, $6.00-8.00. Bakelite one piece push button shaker, $8.00-10.00. Lucite cube, $5.00-7.00.

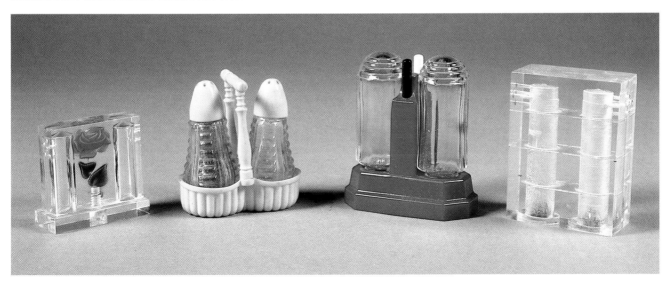

New salt and pepper shakers being made now are rarely repeated. I strongly recommend buying any that appeal unless your collection is primarily one of antiques. If you see something that you really like, particularly if your collection is topical, don't hesitate to buy it. I bought the penguin pulling a trailer in a gift shop last year, and I've never seen it again. New Christmas and other holiday sets come out each year and are not repeated, and promotionals and advertising sets are not usually made again in the same form. A good example of this is RCA Victor, now the Radio Corporation of America. The original Nipper dogs were made by the Lenox China Company; they were followed by a Japanese copy. In the 1950's a plastic Nipper with a gramaphone was made, marked RCA trademark. This year, (1987) I bought

Tomorrow's Collectibles

a ceramic Nipper with gramaphone on a plastic base in the RCA building in New York City. I'm certainly sorry I only bought one pair of the ceramic Statue of Liberty sets at the time of the 100th anniversary of "Miss Liberty." I was so sure they'd would be on sale after all the festivities were over! I have been to myriad souvenir and novelty shops in New York and have not seen a single pair. They seem to have disappeared completely. So don't pass up a new pair assuming that it will be around forever; I've actually seen more pairs of some of the older sets than the new.

TOP: The Cat's Pajamas and Mother Rabbit 1985 & 1983 respectively. These are made by Fitz and Floyd and currently cost $14.95 a pair in Gardenia, a gift shop in Fairfield, Ct. Ray Avery, the owner, was kind enough to lend me the 2 pairs to photograph.

CENTER: Staffordshire Cats on a royal blue base. These are elegant, also made by Fitz & Floyd, and I paid $22.00 for them in December 1986. The Victorian Houses were purchased at the same time, are lighter in weight, less expensive, and have a matching sugar bowl and cookie jar, $10.50. They were made in Japan by Otagiri.

BOTTOM: Two pigs: a pink one and a black and white Hampshire, also Otagiri, $10.50. Cockatoos. These are the same quality as the Stafforshire cats and are very elegant and very Art Deco. Made by Vandor, 1985, $22.00.

TOP: **Two charming pairs of penguins, $10.00-15.00.**

BOTTOM: **Policeman and parking meter (bought at Empire State Bldg gift shop) NYC, $10.00-15.00. An exact copy of the old miniature set; but this is full size and brand new, $10.00-15.00.**

178

TOP: By Vandor, cruising cat & cruising poodle—a take-off on a 1950's set when cars had fins, $12.00-15.00.

CENTER: Shopping cat, bag is marked "Cats Fifth Avenue & has the same logo as Saks Fifth Avenue, $12.00-15.00. Pink poodle wearing sunglasses, sipping a drink and sitting on a "mod" black and white chair, $12.00-15.00.

BOTTOM: Surfer cow by Vandor, note palm tree print on bathing trunks! $12.00-15.00. Sailboat, Ron Gordon design, sails are salt & pepper, $8.00-10.00.

TOP: Cow & beach tube, bikini top, $12.00-15.00. Cow & beach ball by Vandor, $12.00-15.00.

CENTER: Tropical fish by Vandor, luscious colors, $10.00-12.00 pr.

BOTTOM: Dogs with fire hydrant—also a copy of older sets, these are made by Vandor, $12.00-15.00.

ABOVE & CENTER: Ron Gordon design. Chicken & egg. Chicken is attached to tray, egg comes off and splits in half—nicely decorated for Easter, $8.00-10.00 pr.

BOTTOM: Ron Gordon Designs, Inc. English cottage, roof and base are each a shaker, $8.00-10.00.

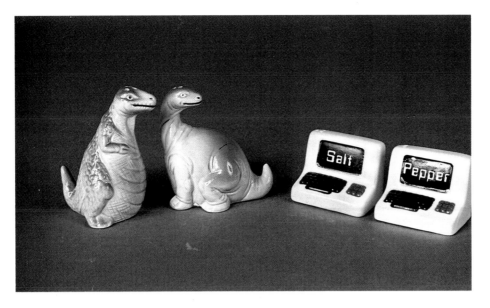

TOP: The old and the new, dinosaurs and computers. The dinosaurs look curious, $8.00-12.00 pr.

CENTER: Fire engine and hat. Law books and gavel. Both these sets are by Sarsparilla, $8.00-12.00 pr.

BOTTOM LEFT: "All I Want For Christmas . . ." This set is also by Sarsparilla, $7.00-10.00.

BOTTOM RIGHT: Zeppelin and hot air balloon, each on its own cloud! $12.00-15.00 (Sarsparilla).

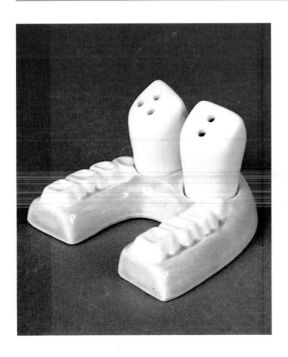

TOP: Piano & stool and juke box are both by Sarsparilla & both very realistic looking, $12.00-15.00.

CENTER: Moon and star by Vandor. These are heavy and beautifully crafted, $15.00-18.00. Helicopter (Sarsparilla) rotor comes off is one shaker, $12.00-15.00.

BOTTOM: Christmas toys, rocking horses and teddy bears by Josefs Originals, $8.00-10.00.

Schroeder's Antiques Price Guide

Schroeder's Antiques Price Guide has climbed its way to the top in a field already supplied with several well-established publications! The word is out, Schroeder's Price Guide is the best buy at any price. Over 500 categories are covered, with more than 50,000 listings. But it's not volume alone that makes Schroeder's the unique guide it is recognized to be. From ABC Plates to Zsolnay, if it merits the interest of today's collector, you'll find it in Schroeder's. Each subject is represented with histories and background information. In addition, hundreds of sharp original photos are used each year to illustrate not only the rare and the unusual, but the everyday "fun-type" collectibles as well -- not postage stamp pictures, but large close-up shots that show important details clearly.

Each edition is completely re-typeset from all new sources. We have not and will not simply change prices in each new edition. All new copy and all new illustrations make Schroeder's THE price guide on antiques and collectibles.

The writing and researching team behind this giant is proportionately large. It is backed by a staff of more than seventy of Collector Books' finest authors, as well as a board of advisors made up of well-known antique authorities and the country's top dealers, all specialists in their fields. Accuracy is their primary aim. Prices are gathered over the entire year previous to publication, from ads and personal contacts. Then each category is thoroughly checked to spot inconsistencies, listings that may not be entirely reflective of actual market dealings, and lines too vague to be of merit. Only the best of the lot remains for publication. You'll find Schroeder's Antiques Price Guide the one to buy for factual information and quality.

No dealer, collector or investor can afford not to own this book. It is available from your favorite bookseller or antiques dealer at the low price of $12.95. If you are unable to find this price guide in your area, it's available from Collector Books, P. O. Box 3009, Paducah, KY 42001 at $12.95 plus $2.00 for postage and handling.

8½ x 11, 608 Pages $12.95